# The Early-~

# Work Force

*A Survival Kit for Hidden Dangers to Your Well Being*

To
/oma
Lotsa love

## Hugh Gilbert

The Larry Czerwonka Company
Hilo, Hawai'i

Second Edition — November 2013

Published by: The Larry Czerwonka Company
Printed in the United States of America

ISBN: 0615906850
ISBN-13: 978-0615906850

# Contents

# Contents

# Contents

# Contents

# Contents

# Foreword by
## Dr. Tony Lynch

Soft tissue disorders are a major cause of worker impairment, functional limitations and disability. These disorders are not a new phenomenon. In 1773, Ramazzine described these disorders:

"Various and manifold is the harvest of diseases reaped by certain workers from crafts and trades that they pursue. All the profit they get is fatal injury to their health, mostly from two causes. The first and most potent is the harmful character of the materials they handle. The second, I ascribe to certain violent and irregular motions and unnatural postures of the body, by reason of which, the natural structure of the vital machine is so impaired that serious diseases gradually develop therefrom."

Most work-related injuries are seen by both the family doctor and/or physiotherapists, chiropractors etc.. The overwhelming majority of these injuries, are musculoskeletal injuries—those involving the nerves, tendons, muscles and supporting structures of the body. While the causes of soft tissue injuries have not been fully elucidated, it is believed these injuries usually involve multiple causes. The World Health Organization has recognized soft tissue disorders as having both *personal* and *work-related* causes.

For an occupational health professional, managing these injuries requires addressing both the medical and occupational factors that may present barriers to an individual returning to work. If these barriers are not dealt with promptly and appropriately, they can lead to significant time loss, and in a proportion of cases, to long term disability. The problem may be further aggravated if the injured worker is only seen by a family doctor or specialist who is not aware of the interplay of factors which influence a worker rejoining his or her company. In the majority of cases, minimal or no intervention is required beyond accommodating the injured worker with temporarily modified transitional duties. Too often workers are re-injured, despite having been through occupational rehabilitation services or having left a job due to the original injury, or in other circumstances both internal and external to work.

The Code of Occupational Medical Ethics of the Canadian Medical Association recognizes the concept of meaningful work as important to a person's well being in both the physical and psychosocial aspects of life. The first paragraph of the Code of Occupational Medical Ethics also states: "[Physicians must] consider first the well being of the employee. Accord the highest priority to the health and safety of the individual in the work place."

However, this position statement, as those in other areas of occupational medicine, can produce ethical dilemmas in choosing between a worker's health and corporate goals. To address these sometimes conflicting goals, one medical association produced a statement entitled, "Early return to work after illness or injury." The guidelines suggest:

"Prolonged absence from work may be detrimental to a patient, and returning to work as soon as possible without endangering the patient's health and safety should be encouraged. An early return to work after an illness or injury (work-related or otherwise) benefits a patient socially and financially. It also preserves a skilled and stable work force for the employer."

This position paper was followed by a similar position paper from another medical association, and the recommendations of these two organizations were adopted by the Canadian Medical Association as a policy. Physicians working in occupational medicine have responsibilities to patients as workers but have constraints placed on them by the priorities of the patients workplace management and environment. Some rehabilitation programs do not always recognize that the body has the potential for self-healing in the first few weeks after an injury. The authors of the CMA policy note :

"Facilitating early return to work by better communication within the work place and treatment centres, including job demand analysis, and work place modification may be of more significance than the actual medical treatment."

The general consensus among occupational health professionals is that facilitating a patient's early return to work through the use of modified duties is possibly the most cost effective intervention they can offer both the worker and employer.

## The Scale of the Problem

During the last 15 years, the number of work accidents has remained fairly stable; however, since 1980 the average cost of claims has risen by 180%. In Canada, a typical employer paid approximately $5,000 per employee towards workers' compensation, disability insurance, and in lost productivity and related expenses. This does not take into account the indirect costs to the injured worker through lost wages and the negative psychosocial effects on the worker and his or her family. In Alberta the number of lost time claims decreased from 37,800 in 1991 to 31,800 in 1995. Paralleling this trend the average of time lost to temporary disability claims dropped from 53 in 1991 to 43.3 in 1995. The fully funded cost per lost-time-claim was $12,700 in 1991 and $11,700 in 1995. However, with the improved economic conditions, the Workers Compensation Board has now seen an increase in new claims and lost time claims reaching a four year high in 1996. The trend has continued into 1997 in most industry sectors. New claims are up 20% and lost time claims have increased by 11% over 1996 numbers. The majority of claims (75%) are in the manufacturing and constructions sectors.

The Economic Burden of Illness in Canada, a 1993 report by Health Canada, attempted to quantify the costs, both direct and indirect, related to illness and injury. The indirect costs were estimated by measuring the present value of lost productivity due to long and short term disability and premature death. Musculoskeletal diseases of all types, and injuries, ranked second and third after cardiovascular diseases. Direct costs were estimated at $2.47 billion and $3.12 billion respectively. Indirect costs were estimated to be $15.33 billion and $11.22 billion, giving total costs (direct and indirect) of $17.79 billion and $14.34 billion. (For cardiovascular diseases this was $19.72 billion). Overall, indirect costs were highest for musculoskeletal diseases (18%), followed by cardiovascular disease (14.5%), and injuries (13.2%).

Similarly, in Britain for 1996, the number of working days lost due to back problems rose fourfold from 1976. Over 80 million days are lost due to registered disability. The cost to the British economy in those years was the equivalent of $12 billion (U.S.). In the U. S. A., in 1989, the annual W. C. B. costs (medical and indemnity payments) due to low back disorders were estimated at $11.4 billion (U.S.) per year. This figure does not include indirect costs such as lost production and the training of new workers. While the number of disability cases appears to be dropping or stabilizing, the individual costs are increasing.

In an attempt to lessen this epidemic, various bodies have enacted primary preventative initiatives for ergonomic standards for the work place. Legislation has been introduced by the government in British Columbia, policy standards have been introduced by individual companies world wide, and, in the U.S.A. new ergonomic standards are being proposed by OSHA (Occupational Safety and Health Administration). The proposed legislation is meeting opposition in Congress because of the potential enormous cost to employers. Merely making ergonomic changes ignores part of the WHO definition of soft tissue disorders as having both *personal* and *work-related* causes. These new standards place the emphasis on *work-related* but ignore the *personal*. From my experience, for ergonomic changes and safe guards to be effective, the workers also need to take some responsibility. Their part in the solution is to take time to make changes in postural habits as explained in the text of this book, to protect themselves and benefit from ergonomic change provided by the company.

Currently, as one means to reduce the number of disabilities in a workforce, pre-employment medical examinations are being tried.

These examinations have proven unreliable in some areas, are fraught with difficulties and can be construed as discriminatory.

**This book may be society's best hope. What Hugh Gilbert,PT, offers to both workers and employers is an insightful and simple book of self help solutions for workers and employers alike.** It gives the work force the tools to identify and minimize existing and potential postural problems which may place them at a high risk of injury and/or disability. For employers, it presents a structured outline of how to determine organizational problems in their individual companies and how to deal with them.

The onus now changes. It is not only on the employer to provide safe working conditions, but also on the workers to make corrections to their postural maladaptations in order to remedy problems and make maximum use of the ergonomic changes in their work environment. The additional advantage for the workers is that they can not only lessen the chances of future injury but can carry over the benefits gained from the program into their home and leisure activities.

~ Dr. Tony Lynch, MD, PhD, ACBOM, CIME, MROCC

At the time of first going to print, Dr. Tony Lynch was the Medical Director for Concept Health, an international organization of occupational physicians. He is certified in occupational and aviation medicine, and is a Canadian/FAA Aviation Medical Examiner. Dr. Lynch resides in Calgary, Alberta.

# *Preface*

This book is the culmination of almost 50 years of experience, first as a student and then as a health care provider. The following people have all been mentors to me, giving me further insight into the cause of injury and disability, not only on the physical level as addressed in this book, but also those who gave insight to care of mental, emotional and spiritual imbalances as part of true healing.

This book was originally self published in 2001 and I thank Larry Czerwonka Company for taking it on board now in 2013 and publishing it. Some of the references therefore are not in terms of todays statistics but the lessons to be learned as as valuable and necessary to the health and wellbeing of the workforce today as they were then.

To recap, firstly I would like to honor Mr. Bill Kinloch P.T. for founding the Scottish Physiotherapy Hospital in Corunna Street, Glasgow, Scotland. He was certainly a man who could be classified as being ahead of his time in the field of Rehabilitative Medicine. His views on kinetics and body mechanics are the foundation of my work. W.H.Fahrne's publications on back care took me further down the road. Dr. M. Rocobado's teachings gave me another piece of the puzzle. Glenda Key P.T. C.E.O. of Key Functional Assessments in Minneapolis, really tied the whole thing into industry for me. Erl Pettman P.T. of Abbotsford, British Columbia, was, to my mind, one of the finest rehab practitioners in North America, and again, was responsible for my ongoing understanding of the kinetic chain. The authors, Robin Sharma, Napoleon Hill, and Dr. Cal Botteril, National Sports Psychologist, were all instrumental in teaching me how to organize and balance the priorities in my life. Kudos to Randy O'Hare, and Dave Brooks of Ipsco Steel, and Rick Cunningham of T.I.W. Western for their vision and proactive attitudes in implementing ground breaking programs for worker safety. Jeff Fraser, of Canada

Post deserves mention for giving me the opportunity to develop my educational program in industry and for supporting me throughout its implementation. To my friends, Leslie Demytruk R.N. in the insurance industry, Mary Mac Gregor P.T. a senior rehabilitation consultant to the Worker's Compensation Board of Alberta, John Rahman, a leading light in orthotics in Calgary, and to Dr.Tony Lynch, Occupational Health Physician, also of Calgary, for his friendship, intuitiveness and informative foreword to this book, many thanks. All of your support and advice has been invaluable. Then there is John Barnes, P.T. whose groundbreaking work in Myofascial Release has completely changed the approach to rehabilitative medicine. Learning this highly skilled craft has been an inspirational journey. My thanks to Kevin Matthews, of Sarnia, Ontario, whose ongoing efforts to educate industry in the effects of fatigue on the workforce, are truly informative and inspiring. To Jackie Green, whose artistic graphics have captured the essence of this book, I extend my thanks and admiration. I know that readers will agree that this young school girl has a unique talent and her future in this field is bright indeed.

To Herman Mueller, Australasian Institute Director, your teachings on human kinetics and psychosomatic therapy should be taken by everyone in rehabilitative medicine.

To my Hawaiian mentors, Rebecca Avery; Papa K; and Kanoa Okalani thanks for holding the light for us all. To James Twyman, thanks for all you have brought to the banquet in the quest for World Peace .To Clay Miller, shamanic visionary from Sedona, Arizona, and Simone Awinha, from Amsterdam, Internationally acclaimed singer, and stage artiste, who have both brought so much clarity and true friendship to me, my deepest thanks.

To my dear friend, true healer, therapist and colleague Mary Felling P.T. of St. Louis, your true friendship and outstanding skill and empathy are just some of the many gifts you bring to my world, and the world of so many others.

And, lastly, to my life and business partner, Jane K. Wardlaw, who has seen me through some tough times with unquestioning support and empathy and who is now finally opening to (and being acknowledged by many for) her own deeply compassionate spiritual healing power and also her powerful warrior energy in balance. It has been a time of vision and wonder together and I will enjoy the rest of the time we have on this path.

This book is dedicated to all of those mentioned—and all I have not recalled—in this preface. I hope that I have met your expectations!

With Thanks and Blessings to you all,
Hugh

# *Introduction*

Many physical complaints and illnesses, often requiring extensive and costly treatment, are now being closely scrutinized, with the potential for increased health care costs to each individual glimmering on the horizon. In the foreseeable future, those who are grossly overweight, with no genetic predisposition; those who abuse alcohol or drugs; and even those who do not exercise regularly, may be held responsible for payment of a large portion of their own health care costs for treatment of conditions incurred as a consequence of their lifestyle. Particularly for smokers, in centers of government and among insurance providers, the idea is evolving rapidly and with growing conviction, that smokers should be responsible for payment of a large portion of their own health care costs. The rationale is that those who smoke are guilty of deliberately inhaling toxins on a regular basis. These toxins have been proven to damage the human body and predispose it to suffering and disability from severe and often fatal lung and heart conditions. The cost of providing care for these conditions is staggering; therefore, the plan is to increase the health insurance premiums of smokers first, to help defray the cost of treatment, and, secondly, to act as a deterrent to smoking for all of society. What this means is that at least for smokers, the individual is now becoming accountable for his or her own health. Health care will no longer accept the full impact of cost for conditions which could possibly have been prevented by a change in living habits.

Our health care systems are overloaded and the emphasis must shift to prevention, by encouraging lifestyle change and accountability. Governments strive to find solutions to spiraling unacceptable cost of treatment. An example of this occurred a few years ago in the United States, where motorcyclists have been lobbying against legislation requiring them to wear helmets while riding their vehicles. The bikers argued that it should be up to each individual whether they wore a helmet or not. The governments of various states apparently agreed with them, but have decided that, should a motorcyclist incur injury from not wearing a helmet, the state is not prepared to bear the cost of treatment. Consequently, bikers were only allowed to ride without a helmet if they could prove that they have adequate health insurance care coverage.

Concern is not confined to governments and health care providers. Many individuals have become increasingly angry that they have to share in the cost of health care for others who knowingly did little or nothing to prevent the problems. For a few years, we had a "Participaction" campaign in Canada.. As a physiotherapist, I applauded the federal government's initiative of that extensive advertising campaign to encourage us all to exercise regularly. This premise collapsed, however, when someone who exercises on a regular basis sustains a "sports injury," meaning sustained time off from work, only to find that he or she can encounter great difficulty in obtaining prompt government-funded treatment of the problem. These people, who have made a conscious effort to stay fit; know that doctors' offices and emergency rooms are filled with a high percentage of patients who have a history of smoking, drug or alcohol abuse, or lifestyle induced obesity, and, therefore, it would seem that those who do not participate in a healthy lifestyle have priority with our health care funding. This is a mixed message we are currently receiving, and the changes on the horizon would appear to be not only practical, but probably long overdue.

The recognized Health care systems in the UK and the USA in particular continue to fail the public and the latest strategies like Obamacare are similarly doomed unless prevention becomes the priority.

While we may or not agree with these sentiments, there is no doubt that the movement towards individual accountability is gaining strength in many countries today and will have a direct impact on each of us and our families in the not too distant future.

It is generally agreed that "bad posture" is a cause of many injuries for which industry, and society as a whole currently bears the cost.

I don't believe in the term "bad posture." In fact, as you will see, the classic military posture of stand up straight, shoulders back, chest out etc is the only true "bad" posture! All posture is simply an adaptation to the stresses being imposed upon the body, so I prefer to use the term Poor Posture as opposed to Bad Posture. Many back injuries can be prevented by use of improved posture. Many neck injuries can similarly be avoided. A high percentage of carpal tunnel syndrome injuries can be completely prevented by the implementation of postural awareness. Proper breathing techniques, practiced regularly, can reduce many bronchial problems and prove beneficial in stress reduction. These are just a few examples where taking responsibility for ourselves would serve us well—especially if we may be held more personally accountable in the future. However, simply saying "watch your posture" is not enough. The causes of those postures need to be identified and diminished, then simple how to tools are needed. Both are provided in this book.

Industry is currently being pressured to recognize the effects of the work environment on its work force, and to make the necessary ergonomic changes in an effort to achieve a decrease in worker injury and disability. As far back as the summer of 2000, the Trade Union Congress (T.U.C.) of Britain, a powerful and influential organization with a membership of over 20 million workers, passed several initiatives to identify hazards in the workplace. The T.U.C. has full government support to make employers more accountable for worker safety.

The T.U.C. also planned to send all members a "body map," an outline of the human body. The plan was for each worker is to mark the areas of his or her body which are painful at the end of each work day. By comparing the *body maps* submitted, managers or medical practitioners from each industry will be able to identify problem areas where symptoms are common or recurrent. With this information available, employers can begin to determine the causes of these ailments and then implement changes to reduce them.

This plan is a huge step forward in work place health and safety, and one which is to be applauded, but which only provides part of the solution. What will inevitably happen, is that workplaces will come under stern scrutiny and many changes will be made. The spotlight must then reverse from the workplace to the worker and the same probing questions will be asked about how fit a worker is to do his or her job and what measures that worker is taking to ensure his or her body is in optimum condition to minimize risk of injury.

In summary, workers will be held accountable for their lifestyles and they will have to drastically reconsider obligations to themselves and others. The responsibility for our own health ultimately lies in our own hands. This is gradually being accepted, and there will come a time when we will be held accountable as individuals for our postural habits, just as smokers are starting to be held accountable today. How would you feel if you were told that your health care premiums were about to increase dramatically because you or one of your children had sustained an injury which could have been prevented by correct posture? This may seem laughable, but many injury claims today are being denied benefits because a pre-existing condition has been found to have contributed to the injury. This in itself is an obscene decision as almost everyone has a pre existing condition of some kind, however it is the current sad reality we have to deal with. It is only a matter of time before poor posture, with all of its ramifications to your body, will be scrutinized as a pre-existing condition, so the potential for increased personal accountability is not as far fetched as some of us might have thought.

Most of us have generally felt quite comfortable with our posture. Some of us have known we have poor posture, but really haven't considered doing much about it. Sure, parents and teachers often told us to quit slouching and sit or stand up straight, but it never really felt comfortable to to sit or stand in this manner, so we didn't give it more than a passing thought.

The problem of poor posture was two- fold. First, some of the people encouraging us to use "correct" posture were misinformed as to what correct posture entailed. For example, not so long ago, school girls were given extra marks in typing tests if they sat properly. The posture for sitting consisted of tucking their feet under their chairs and always, particularly for Catholic schoolgirls, as a matter of strict principle, keeping the knees tightly closed. The cumulative stresses of this *correct* posture on the ankles, knees, hips and low back of the children resulted in a multitude of problems in later life. Often individuals were not aware of the slowly evolving, far reaching consequences of the postures which they regularly used. It doesn't seem fair that they weren't aware they were creating a problem but now are being held accountable, does it? Many injuries could have been prevented if more time had been taken to educate workers and employers on the benefits of good posture and on the cumulative and expensive cost of improper postural adaptations to the work and social environment.

Thousands of people are finding themselves in chronic pain and either unemployed or under-employed, because of cumulative or repetitive injuries which in many cases were totally avoidable. A horrendous and extremely sad scenario is being repeated all too often throughout the industrial world. It is one which has to be addressed immediately if we truly care about our own well being as well as the health of our families, friends, and colleagues.

This book has been written to offer insight into the misconception of correct posture, to give an understanding of what is really causing your "normal" aches and pains, and to offer simple corrective measures. The knowledge gained will enable you to discuss these matters confidently with your family, co-workers, physician, or employer and to enact or demand the changes necessary to improve your health and well being.

# Chapter 1
## The Early-Aging Work Force

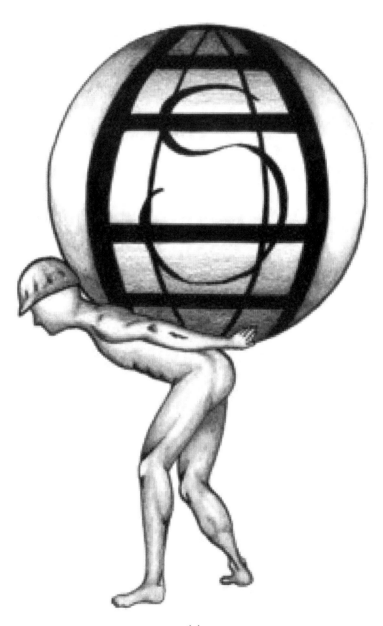

Well before the turn of the century I began to realize the impact of the unseen epidemic I named *The Early-Aging Work Force* and it is relevance has only grown in the Millenium. The information offered here is of paramount importance not only to the Baby Boomers, but to Generation X'ers and beyond. The impact of an early-aging work force affects not only our huge and diverse work force, but also our children in primary and secondary centers of learning on a massive scale as you will come to grasp for yourself as you move through this book. However, you will also come to see how simply it can all be reversed and prevented if we just go to it together.

By the time you have finished this manuscript, you will easily understand how *The Early-Aging Work Force* relates to your life and be well prepared to avoid the causes almost completely. You will also have gained the knowledge and ability to assist your spouse, children and colleagues in having the same skills. The benefits of a healthy, educated and motivated work force will also save incredible amounts in health care costs throughout the industrial world, lowering the costs of your health care and hopefully, as a consequence, the goods and services you purchase!

We are all aware of the inadequacies of our current health care systems and the fiscal pressures on them, and, as industries continue to reduce the size of their work force in effort to achieve increased efficiency. We are all expected to "Do more with less." Physical and mental stresses are spiraling in our work force and burn out is becoming the norm instead of the exception in many industries. Phrases like Repetitive Strain Injury, Cumulative Trauma, Chronic Back Strain,

Stress, Depression and Carpal Tunnel Syndrome have become commonplace. The result is an increasing number of disabled workers. Sadly, most of these workers have accepted their plight as unavoidable and believe their pain and decreased quality of life are simply the by products of aging and/or years of physical labour. Unfortunately this attitude is often reinforced by the opinions of the workers' medical advisors, often even their physicians. In truth, the problem is that the workers' needs are not being properly addressed by the present health care systems, particularly in the areas of rehabilitation and prevention of musculoskeletal disorders. Many workers go through the recognized expensive medical rehab modules not once, but several times, yet still suffer varying degrees of pain and disability. It is my firm belief that many of these cases are **preventable**, while others, if caught in a reasonable length of time, are completely **reversible**.

There is growing evidence that the work force is not satisfied with the inadequacies of our Health Care System and are looking elsewhere for solutions to their problems. In the magazine *Newsweek*, an article entitled "What's Alternative" (November 23, 1998) stated that in 1998 more than 83 million people sought alternative treatment and that 629 million visits were made to these practitioners as compared with only 390 million visits to primary care physicians. These numbers alone are compelling evidence that people no longer accept the quality of health care provided to them and are seeking alternative solutions in ever growing numbers. The trend has only continued and still the message doesn't seem to sink in for some that the current viewpoints on disability and aging are not being accepted any more!

While seeking alternative care is understandable and in many cases successful, it is still a desperate attempt on the part of many people to find someone who can *fix* them. When they do find such a practitioner, they become aware that in many cases they themselves have been (unknowingly) part of the problem due to the postures of their chosen lifestyle, and they come to realize that their recovery is as much dependent on their awareness and willingness to change, as it is on the treatment they are receiving. In other words, the individual is recognizing—usually gladly!—accountability for his or her actions!

In the following chapters you will come to see how your normal aches and pains are not only abnormal, but in many cases **fully avoidable**, without changing your occupation.

**No occupation** is exempt from the hazards of the early-aging process, and poorly chosen physical fitness programs and sports can actually **increase** the incidence of disability. It is vital that you come to understand how to gain control over the symptomatic aging process in your life. We all know that we are getting older, and that aging is a normal and unavoidable process. However, it must be understood that many of the symptoms of aging in the musculoskeletal system are products of postural adaptation to work and social environments, resulting in decreased mobility and function. This erodes your quality of life, and in many cases makes you more susceptible to acute or chronic disability, creating the problem which I define as "The Early-Aging Population." I hope that you will enjoy this book, apply the information offered, and experience dramatic improvements in your quality of life.

A classic example of aging without losing capabilities is seen annually at the Iron Man in Kona, Hawai'i. . . . Sister Mary crosses the finish line under the time limit annually and she is a little catholic nun in her late seventies! What an example to us all. Does that mean we have to be fitness fanatics? If you wish, then go to it! However, for me it shows me how we need to reject the preconceived filters we have in our head—and our society—then discover and eliminate the real causes of our decreased capabilities.

What do I mean when I refer to the category of *The Early-Aging Work Force*? To clarify this concept and show how it evolves, let's say, you, a good worker and valued employee, are injured and have to be off work for a period of time. Most employers and supervisors will wish you a speedy recovery and welcome you back with open arms. So all goes well for a while and then you have a recurrence of your former problem, which again, eventually necessitates time off work. Once more, management is still generally sympathetic, although this time they hope that you "really get fixed up," and in fact often start offering their own remedies if they feel the care you are receiving is inadequate! Grateful for all the help and support, you once again recover and return to your employment. Three months later, oh no! Here it comes again! Desperately, you try to hide the pain and discomfort and try to continue to fulfill you obligations to your employer, your family, and yourself. Ultimately, your performance suffers and you are once again

17

forced to be off work. While your own fear and frustration are growing, along with your discomfort, the management view has often shifted from one of support to one of frustration, sometimes still tinged with sympathy. They feel while you are still an experienced, knowledgeable worker, you are no longer capable of performing your required tasks, and therefore are becoming a liability to their organization and may have to be replaced. Your chronic back, neck, shoulder, elbow, wrist, or chest infection has just made you a part of the *Early-Aging Work Force*! Your future can now become unclear and bleak in a real hurry! Your employer, too, is facing increased costs in the form of Worker's Compensation or Disability costs, possibly loss of productivity, increased overtime costs for other employees plus training of other individuals to fill your shoes. Your physician can also become frustrated as he or she tries to solve the ever tightening circle of pain and disability. If you belong to a trade union, it will generally fight for your benefits and try to find you alternative employment, but this can, unfortunately, often be a prolonged and bitter battle. The point is you are facing a loss of income, and perhaps a premature early retirement, often with minimum pension. And in so many cases, if the worker and management had understood the concepts contained in this book, none of it would have happened!

This does **not** apply only to those who have been doing the same job for over 20 years. Some of the actual cases you will read about have only been doing their particular type of work for less than two years, some only twelve weeks! Imagine being forty- five years old and considered to be part of the *Early-Aging Work Force*. A scary concept. Then consider being twenty years old and given the same label! Now that's terrifying. Not just for the individual, but for the future of Health Care in this nation. The point is that this epidemic is a virtual reality, and it has been my experience that we are losing many of our best and most valued workers in every trade and profession throughout the country. Postural Adaptations are a **huge** factor in this scenario, and I believe the workers themselves are the driving force who can and will ultimately turn this around. The work force is **not** a disposable commodity. They are, for the most part, a dedicated, conscientious skilled and practical group, the virtual lifeblood of our commerce, vital to the functioning of industry, who will implement changes to improve their health **if** the changes make sense to them. That is why I am confident that, if these concepts are clearly defined, those who read them will implement the preventative measures, and, when the benefits are realized, will in fact take responsibility for teaching others.

Management must also realize the *Early-Aging Work Force* is a real phenomenon. They are aware the current costly methods of care have not solved the problem. They too can and will examine and use the principles of change advocated here, because they will come to realize that these principles will benefit their personal lives as much as their employees', with obvious benefits to the personal and corporate environment.

So the *Early-Aging Work Force* has come about primarily and simply as a result of postural maladaptations we have unknowingly made in our homes and work environments!

In Chapter Two we will look at the first obvious example of a major cultural adaptation to a detrimental posture, one for which the cumulative effects are well known.

# Chapter 2
# Sit and Feel Good

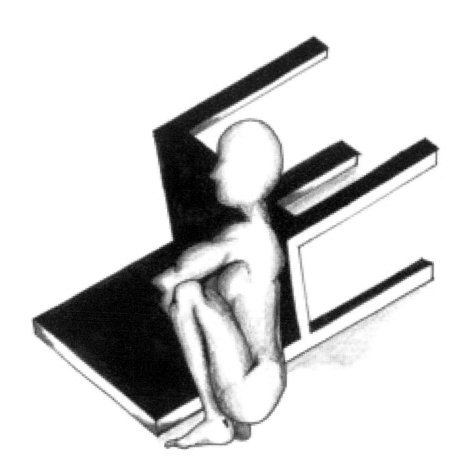

My experience in Rehabilitative Medicine for over forty five years as a physical therapist has truly made me aware how we humans are creatures of habit and have the capacity to adapt to our environment. What I didn't fully realize until relatively recently, was the impact these adaptations have on our future well being and how these same adaptations, which seem to help us survive in our chosen environment, are really harmful (so we'll call them maladaptations) and are becoming the very cause of disabling us, making us a part of an *Early-Aging Work Force* with the often terrifying consequent loss of health, income, and self-esteem. Before we get into some specifics which influence our daily occupation, it is important to examine some cultural beliefs which have a huge impact on our well being.

Let's start with one we are all familiar with: **sitting in a chair**. You're probably doing it right now and chances are, it **feels good**, otherwise you wouldn't be doing it. We know it is bad for us. It has been well known and preached for many years that sitting for prolonged periods is detrimental to our spines, muscles, ligaments, and circulation, but we keep doing it because, not only do we have no alternative, but it **feels good**. We understand, but we continue spend more than a fair share of our time in this position.

Sitting began as a status symbol many centuries ago and has become ingrained in the fabric of our lives, although it is a posture totally alien to the form and function of the human body. Originally, the chair was just a higher platform on which the most important members of society stationed themselves. If you think about animals, such as wolves, where the alpha male (and female) take, and if necessary, defends the highest piece of ground against any other would be leaders, and human games such as King of the Castle, you'll understand the original function of the chair. Gradually, leaders of society gave chairs to those in their favor to affirm their status, although these chairs were not as large or as high as the leaders'.

This system probably spread through societies, with husbands and fathers giving themselves raised platforms or chairs to show that they were the head (at least in their own minds) of their household.

Gradually women and children also obtained status, but not as large or as high as dad's.

If you don't think this is still relevant in today's society, then look around your own home or work place. Better still, walk into any furniture store and look at the dining room suites for sale. How many still have the end chairs higher backed that the rest? Who generally sits in these? The head of the household, right? So, from the Queen of England's throne to the everyday household, seating is still about power, and despite the postural inadequacies, has not only become accepted, but **feels good** most of the time, which is a classic example of **postural adaptation to our environment**.

Documentation is available on indigenous peoples who have no word for "backache" in their vocabulary. Wouldn't it be great if it were true for us? Most of us have seen documentaries on programs such as National Geographic in which, when tribesmen meet they do not sit, but squat comfortably with their buttocks touching their heels and their arms resting on their knees. In this position, their spines are in almost perfect alignment. They are, as we were, functionally suited for this comfortable posture, and in fact, these people have a pad of fat behind the knees to help provide comfort and endurance in this position. We, however, in western society, no longer have this pad of fat as it no longer has a purpose to us. Our bodies have evolved to our work and home environment, with prolonged use of chairs no longer necessitating squatting. Try it for yourself. Most of us will find that attempting to achieve and maintain this position is quite difficult and can be humorous to observe.

Chairs are not the only cause of postural dysfunction, but no one can deny their contribution. Neither must we give up our chairs and revert to squatting. This is simply an example of how we have adapted to what has become a postural necessity in our homes, transport, and in many cases our work sites, and, despite the fact the human animal was built for mobility and flexibility, we have not only accepted the prolonged use of this posture, but have conditioned ourselves into the notion that most of the time it feels good even though it is in fact highly detrimental over an accumulated period of time. The aches, pains and disabilities which can and do occur from this activity, can precipitate us into the dreaded *Early-Aging Work Force*.

There is also another potentially devastating effect of prolonged sitting which we have not been aware of and one which you will come to understand by the end of this book. We will therefore be looking at sitting again more closely later on.

Many excellent publications are available about improving your posture while sitting and also on how to apply ergonomics to your desk and chair, but, obviously, you should get up and walk around as much as possible, and see your health professional to learn regular stretches you can perform at work or at home. Remember your muscles, ligaments, and joints have altered to suit your prolonged use of this posture, and these adaptations can eventually harm you in either your work or social environment. Then, if these adaptations are still not addressed, the injury can recur again and again, with ever increasing debilitating effect.

So, knowing what you know now, put this book down and get up and walk around for a minute or two, or if you feel really ambitious, get up and stretch!

The obvious question here is, "How do I stretch?" The answer is, do whatever feels like it needs to be done! Let your body tell you what to do. The human body is quite capable of initiating stretches to the areas needing attention, if we just pay attention to it. Let your body show you what it needs and move and stretch whatever feels right, whether it is your back, neck, arms, legs or wrists (or all of these!). If you listen to your body and slowly move into stretches which feel good, your chances of injuring yourself are extremely low. If however, you don't trust yourself enough to do this then, do consult your health professional for a regular stretching routine that can easily be performed at work and at home.

# Chapter 3
# Real Men Don't Breathe!

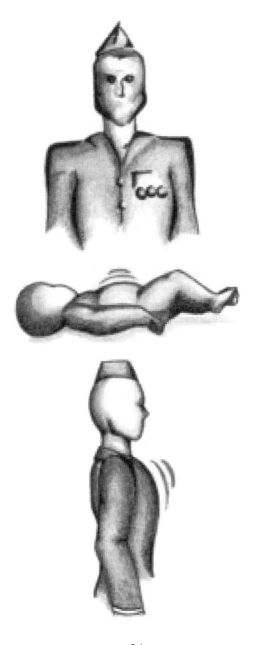

The next *harmful posture* which is deeply rooted in the beliefs of Western Society, is standing! Every time we try to *stand straight* as taught in Western Society, we are restricting our ability to breathe! I can hear you say: "I've been breathing all my life and standing for a good amount of time too and I've never given it a thought. I must be doing it okay because I'm still here." True, but let's take a moment and consider the following. Who, traditionally, has been our societies postural hero and role model over the last 2,500 years? The warrior, correct? From the Ancient Greeks and Romans to the twentieth century, being a man has meant being a warrior, standing at attention, feet together, chest out, armed with shield and spear or rifle and bayonet. **This** is what a man should be! **This** is what women idolize(or at least that's the implication)! The message is deeply rooted in our culture, and is still relevant today. If you doubt that, subconsciously, we still subscribe to this then picture, for example, a group of men standing together, relaxed and talking together in a lounge bar. One or more attractive ladies then enter the establishment and proceed to walk toward this group of men. Watch how, having noticed the appearance and approach of the ladies, the gentlemen rapidly, and, hopefully unnoticed, suck in their abdomens, stick out their chests, draw their shoulders back (almost in full military stance) and desperately try to make eye contact. The ladies, however, are only passing through the lounge on their way to the restaurant, and are quickly gone, at which point the men relax into their former happy slouches and debate which of them the recent passers by couldn't resist! We've all see this type of scenario, and if we're honest, gentlemen, we have to admit that at some time or another, we've all done it!

The military posture is one which we have accepted more than we realize. Any one who has been in the military can verify that standing at attention is neither natural nor comfortable, but there is another effect which contributes to the *Early-Aging Work Force*.

What is the format for the old military posture? As Sergeant Majors throughout the ages have roared menacingly to their recruits: "Shoulders back! Chest out! Stomach in! Breathe, Man, Breathe!" Or words to that effect, right? Most of us, when someone, a physician for example, asks us to take a deep breath, do it in exactly that manner whether we have been in the military or not. So what's wrong with that?

Let's begin with a little basic anatomy. Your rib cage protects and moves to accommodate the vital organs it contains. The shape of the rib cage can be thought of as a bird cage, and the floor of that cage is a dome -shaped muscle, called the diaphragm. Inside this cage are three major organs. These are, two very large, pear shaped, lungs, with the heart in between and mostly protected by your breast bone. The lungs extend all the way from your collarbones to the floor of the cage, and are capable of large intakes of air. Now, if we breathe in the "military" fashion in our normal daily routine, never mind when we deliberately take a deep breath, what happens? We generally use only the top half (some would say less) of our lung capacity to get oxygen into our system! That big domed shaped muscle is supposed to flatten out, allowing the lungs to expand, but it can't due to the Military Model thinking! Therefore, as our bodies thrive on oxygen, we seldom, if ever, getting adequate ventilation! Any alarm bells going off yet?

Let's proceed and see what happens next.

For example, what if we live and/or work in a polluted environment? I don't think there is any argument left that the air we breathe is not as pure as it was twenty years ago. We may debate just how bad it is, we may argue fiercely over who or what is to blame, but I think it is generally accepted that we inhale pollutants to varying degrees every day of our lives. So, here we are, inhaling tiny harmful particles and where do those which are not absorbed, go?

Gravity gradually lets them settle towards the seldom used base of the lungs. Now let's add cigarettes to the mix and the problems multiply. Don't kid yourself, you don't have to be a smoker and/or work in a hazardous environment to be at risk. Every day pollutants can gradually create a build up of dust and toxins in your lungs.

I think you can now see how this will almost certainly make you a part of the *Early-Aging Work Force*. Consider the employee who, for the first time, has to take time off work due to a chest infection. He recovers and returns to the job. However, the infection never really clears up and two months later he is unable to go to work again. Now his colleagues and superiors are offering their own remedies, and sometimes he even tries them. Almost recovered, he returns to work again, having exhausted his medication and his tolerance for being stuck at home, but alas, within a relatively short time, is again confined to bed.

As you now know, this is the point where the employer may start to wonder if he still has an effective employee or, often with regret, considers finding a replacement! What can we do to minimize the cumulative effects of pollutants and help fight infection? Get more air into our lungs on a regular basis immediately and with as many breaths as possible wont hurt, correct?

Here's how. Recall how a baby breathes and picture it. See the little tummy rise and fall? That's how it should be done, using your diaphragm. Babies do it, wind instrument players and singers do it, those who practice yoga, meditation and relaxation do it, but the rest of us don't. That is our problem and here lies our solution.

Think of what happens when we breathe naturally and not contrived. On inspiration—in breath—the diaphragm should almost flatten out. This greatly increases the area of the cage we spoke about, and allows air to rush in and fill the lungs all the way to the bottom. Then, when we exhale, we help the body push those unwanted particles back up towards the top of the lungs again, instead of having them gathering at the base.

How to do it:

Sitting comfortably, run your index finger down your breastbone until you get to the little pointed part at the bottom. You'll know when you're there, as your fingers will suddenly feel soft resistance as opposed to the hard resistance of your breast bone. Done that? Okay, don't move your finger—and don't press hard—that's the first step.

Now, with your other hand, measure down three more finger widths, and stop there. You can remove the first finger now. That's step two. Okay, here we go! When you breathe in, slowly and deeply try to make your tummy come out and push your fingers away. Remember push out only on the **in** breath, and then just let the air come out of your mouth—don't force exhale—and let your tummy relax as you do so. Try five to ten of these in a row right now, before reading further.

If you found it difficult, stay with it and keep trying. Your body knows how to do it, and just needs to be reminded.

For the rest of you, how many felt a little light-headed? Quite a few, I'll bet. To those of you I say, "Well done, you've got it!" What, in effect, happened to you is that your bodies just received much more oxygen than you are used to, and you went on an oxygen high (which only lasts for a couple of seconds). Your body quickly puts the oxygen to good use in your system and would really like you to do that more often.

When some of you were doing this exercise it made you cough, didn't it? That's great! That's the body's way of getting rid of the debris in your lungs, so you've already started to help improve your health. It's as easy as that.

There is another benefit of taking even a few breaths in this manner, every day. Most of us, towards the end of our work day, start to feel fatigued and have increased muscle tension in various parts of our bodies. Many of us also have our "normal" tired and painful neck and shoulders, right? With this combination it's easy to see how, at this time of day, we are much more prone to making mistakes in our designated job and are, unfortunately, at a higher risk of injury. Here's where you can put this exercise to the test. Even a few properly performed deep breaths will increase your mental alertness and the increased oxygen supply to your muscles will decrease the build up of tension in them. The benefits will be almost immediate.

Another good time to practice this technique is going to and from work when you're stopped at a red light. Two or three deep breaths there will be gratefully appreciated by your body, and soon you will in the habit of doing it regularly. You won't have to keep *marking the spot* with your finger. Once you have practiced diaphragmatic breathing a few times, you can do it discreetly and easily without using your finger as a marker.

How many of us go through life feeling constantly tired? If we're not getting enough oxygen, how could we feel any other way?

So, there's your first lifestyle change. Are you being asked to give up your present lifestyle or career? No! Is this going to restrict your activities in any way? No! All that is asked of you is to give this kind of breathing a try. To combat our current lifestyles and polluted environment, you now have a powerful yet simple tool which can make a dramatic difference to your life. **You have control** and can start taking steps to improve the quality of your life, while also lessening the odds of your becoming part of the *Early-Aging Work Force*.

[note: for those of you suffering from acute stress and or fatigue there is another factor to be addressed but it is not for this book to address. If this is you then please connect with me in person and I will explain further at **yahugh@journeysend.ca**] So, now before moving on the next chapter, take five proper deep breaths now. Feel better? So maybe you could get up and walk around the room two or three times and stretch?

Lets take a look at how our everyday postures can and do, often unknowingly, affect every aspect of our lives because, even though they are detrimental to our health, they actually "feel good" to us!

As an example, consider the **Coal Mining** industry, a physically demanding job performed by a well respected group of men. When most of us think of an older, retired miner, we picture a proud elderly gentleman, walking somewhat stooped over and in some ways physically broken from a lifetime of extremely hard labor. The risks of gases, dust, long hours, and physical danger, are well known. Alas, the repetitive postures required in their tasks also proved to be an overlooked contributing factor in their almost inevitable disability.

In my youth in Scotland, the coal industry was still booming. The miners worked long, hard, dangerous work weeks, and there was something else they had a passion for. Lawn bowling! These tough, hard working men had a passion for lawn bowling? Every colliery had its own bowling green and woe betide anyone who was not a union man who stepped on the sacred turf. The collieries vied with each other, not just for the best team, but also for the best playing surface. Huge trophies were battled for, annually.

Can you picture any other similar group of men, involved in high risk activities, such as rig workers, steel workers, or rodeo riders indulging in lawn bowling as their favorite past time? It struck me as an unusual and almost inappropriate passion for this particular group of young men. Then, gradually I began to make the connection. In what position do miners spend much of their time while working at the coal face, drilling, lifting, and loading? Bent over! What position had their bodies adapted to as being the most comfortable? What position were they in, in their favorite sport? Bent over! So, there it was, the classic example of a postural adaptation being carried over into the social environment, so not only were they in poor posture for the 40 to 60 hour work week, but they might spend up to another 15 to 20 hours "comfortably" lawn bowling, or their other passion, Gardening!

The miners I spoke to defended the tradition of lawn bowling and gardening in their "allotments" vigorously and proudly until I asked why they did it. Their reply was usually, "Because my father and his father before him did it." My next question was, "And what happened to them?" Now you could see understanding beginning, as their forefathers had been bent and, to varying extents, disabled long before their time. The current generation had never thought that their fate could be any less. They seemed to accept it with an almost proud stoicism. Until now. Suddenly, they were interested in what they could do to alter the future they had previously thought of as inevitable. For those who reduced the hours they were lawn bowling/gardening and got into different activities, the results were obvious within the first few weeks.

I remember suggesting they take up tennis, an idea that met with derision. "We don't play tennis." "That's not a sport for REAL men" (remember this was still the sixties). My answer was, "Fair enough, but that's a wee bit strange, since lawn bowling isn't exactly a contact sport either!" Again, there was instant recognition of the message I was sending.

These men were among the first I knew who realized that all jobs create harmful adaptive postures, but the real danger is adapting to these postures and using the exact same postures unknowingly **(because they feel good)** in their home and social activities. How many of you working in **Building Construction,** or **Landscaping** crews, moving materials etc, or **Warehouse** staff loading/unloading product, or in **Elderly Care/Nursing homes,** or **Nurses/Hospital staff** lifting and transferring patients, have accepted that back and neck pain are your normal, and enjoy recreational activities such as ten pin bowling, curling, or gardening? Do you understand now what is happening to your body? How much time per week do you REALLY spend in some degree of a bent over (flexed) posture?

The ongoing effect of the use of these job- related postures was obvious to these miners, and they set about changing this, by countering with different posture when away from the coalface, and began enjoying activities such as rugby, soccer, swimming—and even tennis!—with quickly noticeable results which not only affected their present quality of life, but greatly reduced their chances of becoming a part of the *Early-Aging Work Force*.

In the case studies in the pages ahead, you will see how all occupations produce some form of modified posture, which carries over into every facet of life. Identifying these postures and applying simple remedies, is the key to the work force having control of their physical health and to giving them hope, not just for less discomfort in their lives currently, but hope for a healthy, enjoyable, timely retirement.

Take time again now to get up and walk or stretch a little. Then sit back down and take five **proper** deep breaths before continuing.

# Chapter 5
# Disabled While You Sleep?

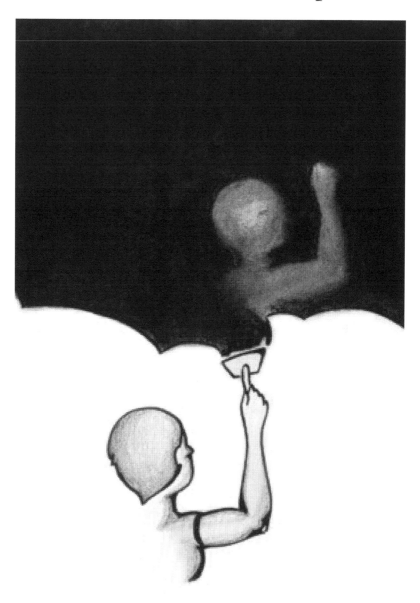

We've now looked at the problems associated with some of our regular habits, such as sitting and breathing. At this point you might be thinking, "I'm going to bed. Surely he's not going to tell me that's bad for me too?" Well, guess what? Before you slip off to dreamland, maybe you should read just one more chapter. I think you'll be glad you did.

While sleeping is nature's way of replenishing the human body and preparing it for the next day's work load, there are some very real and avoidable dangers which can greatly affect your ability to keep performing your required duties, and which can in no small way contribute to your becoming one of the *Early-Aging Work Force* statistics.

Do you sleep on your stomach or know someone who does? This is aimed directly at you! Those who sleep on their stomach keep health professionals like me in business! Sooner or later these people need our help and, they'll keep coming back, as their problems recur again and again. While repeat business is a great thing in most industries, it gets frustrating for both us and you when you keep coming back to get "fixed up." It's like you're always getting tune ups when your body craves an overhaul, isn't it? The secret is to firstly come to understand what you've been doing to your body (if you didn't know, how could you stop?). Then, by taking the simple steps to change or alter the stresses on your body, you will create an environment where your rehab practitioner has a chance at giving you long term relief. Sleeping on the stomach is done by so many people because it "feels good." It must, or they wouldn't be doing it. The best way to demonstrate how absurd this position is, simply read on and then just do it or instruct someone else to do it (while you read) in the following steps. The results will be obvious, and probably more than a little comical. So see if you can get someone (preferably someone who does not normally sleep on his or her stomach) to play along.

Step One: Lie face down on the floor with your arms at your sides. *Well, this isn't going to last long is it? Firstly your low back is sagging, but more importantly, you can't breathe! But okay, move on.*

Step Two: "Alright, I'll let you breathe. Turn your head to the right. *Great! Now you can breathe, but your lower back is still sagging, and now you've twisted your neck to 90 degrees." Are you going to stay in this position all night??*

Step Three: Okay, okay! I know that's not comfortable, so we'll put a pillow under your head. Go ahead grab a pillow. *Ah! That's a bit better. Now your back is sagging, your head is twisted to 90 degrees, and the pillow just put a curve in your neck to add to the twist!*

Before going to step four, recall the chapter on breathing. Suppose we have someone who doesn't breathe properly, smokes cigarettes, and now spends eight hours a night lying on his or her rib cage so it can't expand! A recipe for disaster? If you think so, you're catching on. If not, go back and read it again!

Step Four: Bring your right arm up to rest on the floor with your elbow level with your shoulder. *Now we're talking, aren't we? Your lower back sags, your rib cage can't expand, your neck is twisted and bent at 90 degrees, and you've jammed your right shoulder (where your collar bone joins your shoulder).* This joint is so important, you will read several references to it in future chapters.

We're not finished yet. To achieve the ultimate in "comfort" in this position, there's one more step!

Step Five: Bring your right knee out and up along the floor until it is parallel with your hip. There You Go! *Now you can sleep. Your lower back sags, your rib cage can't expand, your neck is twisted and bent at 90 degrees, you've jammed your shoulder, you've jammed your right hip into its socket, and you've twisted your pelvis! And you're going to stay in this position for 25 to 33% of your life? But it feels good!*

Have your muscles and ligaments adapted to this posture and accepted it as normal? Could those adaptations eventually create problems in other areas of your life? The answer is . . . they already have!

The scale of this problem and its effects on our population are staggering. Frequently I'm asked by people who have **figured out the problem**, "How do I stop, I've been sleeping on my stomach for years?" Some people say, simply put a tennis ball on your stomach and wrap it there with a towel or sheet, so that when you roll on your stomach the ball will make your life uncomfortable, and you will return to the side lying posture. My purpose is not to belittle this well-meant advice. However, it has been my experience that a lot of tennis balls have been bounced off walls, furniture, spouses, family pets and windows, and the thrower has returned to his "comfortable" position on his stomach for a good night's sleep. What I recommend is this. Every time you become aware that you are sleeping on your stomach, roll onto your side. Don't lose sleep over this. The habit of years will not be broken overnight, but will persist, until your body gradually, comes to appreciate the new position and accept it. The feedback I have had over a two to three month period, would indicate the effectiveness of this approach.

Here is a relevant case study which will show a clear example of how these postural adaptations can precipitate us into the *Early-Aging Work Force*:

Subject: Valued employee Age: 23;

Occupation: **Plasterer/Dry Waller**

Problem: No longer able to perform duties

History: Hard worker, lots of overtime, 5 years experience.

Developed problem with right shoulder—-2 weeks work loss. Three months later, recurrence of shoulder problem—7 weeks work loss. Two months later, recurrence of shoulder problem—laid off—replaced on the work force, and his shoulder was not recovering!

On taking the subject's history, I understood how this otherwise fit and healthy young man was angry, frustrated, and obviously afraid for his future. We took a closer look at what had happened here. In his job, he holds the plaster in a hod in his left hand and slaps it on the drywall with a trowel held in his right hand. He stated that most of the work he did was at shoulder height and above.

This worker's elbow was in a position of 90 degrees to his shoulder for the better part of the 50 hour work week. Do you think his muscles and ligaments might have come to accept this position as normal?

While he was sitting in his chair, talking to me, he had his hands clasped behind his neck! What position is his shoulder in? Remember how the miners adapted to their work posture? To cap it off, he mentioned that over the last two to three years, he had found it more comfortable to sleep on his stomach. If you don't see where I'm going with this, look back to Step Four in the face down sleeping procedure. His arm is in this position for another 40 to 50 hours per week! The accumulated effect of this "comfortable" (habitual) posture on this young man's shoulder became obvious. Once he understood it, he (1) started doing daily stretches to counteract this posture, and (2) gradually stopped sleeping on his stomach.

Result: Two months later, he was re-employed and, at a six month follow-up, had had NO recurrence of his symptoms.

Key Element: The worker *figured it out* and *took control*.

## Chapter 6

# Carpal Tunnel – A Twist
# of the Wrist?

Carpal Tunnel Syndrome: one of the foremost causes of physical disability of the 90's. Tens of thousands of workers have it, tens of thousands more are painfully and silently developing it, and the numbers of people on the disabled work force because of it are rising steadily. What is it and can you prevent it? I'll explain the former in a minute or two, but as for the question of whether or not you can prevent it, the answer is Yes! Read on and discover how.

Before I begin, I have to offer my thanks and respect to Glenda Key, P.T., of Key Functional Assessments Inc. of Minneapolis, who, as far back as the late 1980's, had identified the problem and was successfully implementing reduction and prevention programs in the work place. Glenda also taught me the basis of what I now know.

First, where is and what is the carpal tunnel? Turn your hand palm up toward you. Don't use the hand you wear a watch on or you won't be able to follow from here. Actually your watch strap is probably covering the carpal tunnel exactly! Begin by bending your hand forward, toward you, and keep it there. Now look at your wrist. See those creases? That's it! You're looking at it. That's the carpal tunnel. It's an oblong -shaped box area between those creases. Three sides of the box (i.e., the back and sides of your wrist) are made of bone. The lid, or front side (the one you're looking at) is a ligament completing the box. Passing through this "box" are all of the tendons which make your fingers move. Wiggle your fingers and you can probably see those tendons all the way up your forearm. Blood vessels and nerves, particularly one called the Median nerve, also pass through the "tunnel" to your hand and fingers. The bones of the wrist, or what you might think of as the floor of the box, are called the carpal bones, and the ligament on top completes the tunnel for everything passing through it. Thus the Carpal Tunnel is formed. While certain medical conditions predispose a person to Carpal Tunnel Syndrome, if we overuse any of our muscles they become swollen. Similarly, if we repeatedly perform the same motion, then strain of a cumulative nature will result, hence the terms we hear so often, *Overuse, Cumulative,* or *Repetitive Strain Injury.* When we overuse the muscles in our wrist, the tendons, of course, will become inflamed and swollen. The problem is that they are confined in the Carpal Tunnel and they start to constrict each other as well as the median nerve and blood vessels, creating further inflammation. Now the problem really picks up speed. Glenda Key was one of the first to realize it's not just overusing the muscles that creates the problem, but physically and repeatedly making the Carpal Tunnel smaller, which is the real trigger to this one! How do you make the space smaller? There are two easily identifiable and common examples. Okay, look at the palm of your hand as you did before. Now bend you hand towards you again. See how the creases become more and more evident. That's because you are constricting the front part of the tunnel. This movement is called flexion. Now, let your hand relax again, still palm up. Without moving your arm, moving only your wrist, move your hand and wrist inward toward your body in a chopping motion, and keep it there. See how your wrist is squished on the one side (your little finger side)? That's the second constrictive position. This position is called ulnar deviation. Some of us already know we do this frequently and are trying to change things. Some of us know we do this and haven't been able to do a thing about it. Some of you don't believe you ever do it at all! I think I can change your minds.

Case Study: **Professional Golfers** with Carpal Tunnel Syndrome!

Put your hands in the position of holding your golf club. Now look at your hands. Is that deviation? So here are these golfers, using this posture hour upon hour, day upon day, month upon month. Think there's a potential problem here? Of course there is. So when these ladies and gentlemen asked what they could do, they were told to cut back on using that posture. They, of course, refused to do so, stating that this was their livelihood. Wouldn't we all have said the same? You don't have to give up golf or whatever you do when you are working, simply don't do it when you're not working. In other works, give your wrists a rest!

The golfers were a bit confused and doubted they ever put their wrists in that position when they weren't golfing. They were asked then to put their hands on the steering wheel as if to drive their cars, and—there it was again! How about cleaning your teeth? Combing or shampooing your hair? Turning a key in the lock? Lifting a coffee cup? Doing housework? Using the channel changer? By minimizing the times they were in this posture in the home and social environments, their tendons had a chance to heal, as they were not constantly constricted, and they were able to return to their chosen profession with a few ongoing stretches. Once again, when the workers [athletes] figured it out and took control of the situation, they were able to solve it and stay gainfully employed in their chosen career and sport!

Case Study: **Poultry Plant Processing Workers**, with Carpal Tunnel Syndrome.

Touring two of these plants helped me understand the problem. What I saw was the mostly female work force, working on the production line. Most of them worked with their wrists in a constant flexion and deviation, and their numbers of workers off work with Carpal Tunnel Syndrome were rising rapidly. One of the companies then proposed a solution. They had noticed, that while some men in their employ also had the symptoms, the percentage of female workers with the problem was significantly higher. Therefore, they were considering laying off all the female workers and employing only males! Now, I cannot comment on the issue of gender susceptibility, but I have examined and treated many men with this problem in other industries, so I'm not convinced of this generalization.

Anyway, back to the women poultry plant workers. We established that there was almost constant use of flexion and deviation. What we need to add to this, is that these ladies then go home, peel potatoes, open tinned food, stir food while cooking it, feed the family, clear the dishes, wash the dishes, put the dishes away, bath the kids, tuck them into bed, do a load of laundry, dust, vacuum, polish, and go to bed. They get up in the morning and do a lot of it again, and then they go to work. This is just a selection of the chores these ladies were doing on a daily basis. Pretend that you are doing any of the activities mentioned above and check your wrist position. What do you see? Flexion, deviation, or a combination of both? So, apart from the constant compression of the carpal tunnel at work for 40 to 50 hours a week, how many more hours a day were their wrists in these positions? Do you think their life got easier on weekends? Not a bit. Therefore, their wrists were taking a constant beating between their home activities and their occupation. Any surprise that chronic inflammation resulted? (Most of the male workers did not have the same domestic responsibilities, therefore their wrists were getting rest when at home!)

Now, these women couldn't control their work environment, but once they recognized that flexion and deviation were major contributors to the problem, they could minimize the damage in the home environment by altering their wrist position to avoid these postures. [more about how they did this in later chapters] Finally they were giving their wrists a rest from the constant compression.

In the meantime some of their employers had spent large sums of money altering the work site into a more ergonomically acceptable environment, and they tried to set up schedules of job rotation so that their workers could alternate tasks throughout the work day. This is commendable action and certainly is helping, but not eradicating the problem. You should be able to figure out why by now.

First, the women were unaware of the specific positions contributing to the problem and were still heavily involved in their use in the home environment. Secondly, management were unaware of the specific positions contributing to the problem and while they had proactively implemented a rotating schedule of alternate tasks to minimize repetitive work, what they didn't grasp was that some of the alternate tasks still involved flexion and or deviation! With these factors will the problem ever go away? No, plain and simple.

Worker education is the only basis from which a real end to this problem can evolve. I have stated this over and over again, when the worker understands it, the problem begins to be solved.

Before we move on to another example in the work force, let's make sure we've got it clear. If you walk up to a wall and hit your head against it, you'll get a lump on your head, right? So, you go to the doctor and ask him to fix it. He will tell you to ice it and everything should heal in time. So off you go, put ice on the lump, then walk up to the same wall and hit your head again! The pain and swelling get worse and you go back to your physician and tell him his advice isn't working. Sounds ridiculous, doesn't it? But if you didn't realize that banging your head against the wall was the problem, you wouldn't be able to prevent it from recurring. Similarly, if workers don't realize that repetitive flexion and deviation are contributing towards the problem, how can they be expected to stop, and how can treatment be effective for any length of time?

A classic example of this is the worker with Carpal Tunnel Syndrome, who is off work and in constant pain, with medication no longer effective and facing surgery. What the surgeon has said he or she will do, in effect, is simple and effective. Remember the ligament or "lid" across the top of the box of the carpal tunnel? Your surgeon will simply snip one end of it, lift it up and lay it back down without securing it too tightly. This will take the pressure off the tendons underneath. The results are usually excellent and logical. The problem is that over time, scarring in the tissues and exercise may gradually tighten the ligament up again to some degree. The real problem is, if the worker continues to *bang his or her head against the wall* by continued flexion and deviation, it's a matter of time before the problem recurs, resulting in the same cycle of pain, disability, and possible surgery. This tends then to reflect poorly on the health professions, who have tried in vain to stop the problem, but now *you know* that the quality of care you received was probably excellent, but was doomed to fail because the only person who could change things was you! Again, this is evidence that with the worker understanding the problem can be solved.

It is worth repeating that the women in the poultry plant were going home to the "**Housewife**" activities mentioned with ongoing stress and strain on their wrists, while the men (traditionally) were going home to hit the couch and control the channel changer! Whose wrists were getting a rest?

There are ways to help the worker remember to alter their posture, and we'll get to those later.

This Syndrome is not industry specific, and we've already discussed golfers and poultry workers. Here's another example:

Case Study: **Cashiers/Check Out** workers in the food industry.

Have you ever been stuck in the slowest moving line in the supermarket? If not, and you want to try it, follow me around the store and pick the same check-out line I do. It never seems to fail, I never get in the fast lane no matter how much time I take reviewing the possibilities. Anyway, the next time you're stuck in the line up, pay close attention to the cashier's hands. While lifting, scanning, and bagging the groceries, her hands are almost continuously in *flexion and/or deviation*. The food industry is genuinely attempting to minimize the incidence of Carpal Tunnel Syndrome by spending large amounts of money and time in redesigning the check-out counters, yet the problem persists. I have heard many cases of employees who only work twelve to fifteen hours a week, who have developed Carpal Tunnel Syndrome! If we look a little closer at these workers' home and social activities, we will find they are similar to the poultry workers, and will certainly find ongoing flexion and deviation. In the vast majority of cases, once the employee understands the causes, it's a sure bet he or she will do something about it. *Now* the treatments being given to those already suffering will have a chance of ongoing success. *Now* there is real hope of prevention in those who are at high risk, but have not yet developed the symptoms. *Now* the workers will finally have some control over whether they joining the *Early-Aging Work Force!*

Some other examples of high risk occupations are **Office Workers,** particularly those using the mouse with their computer; **Carpenters/Joiners** using saws and hammers, etc.; **Welders, Bricklayers, Electricians, Glaziers, Carpetlayers, Roofers,** all using the tools of their trades, **Truck Drivers/Bus Drivers** with hands on steering wheel plus gear shifting; **P**ainters/**Decorators** using brushes; **Homemakers** doing housework; **Nurses/Health Care Workers** lifting patients and making beds; **Cake Decorators, Waitresses, Airline Stewardesses** carrying heavy trays of food, **Hairdressers, Baggage Handlers** all **Production/Assembly line** workers; **Heavy Equipment Operators**; all workers where the job entails lifting and carrying , and the list just goes on and on, with the number of people at risk moving into millions!

To see if you've really grasped *flexion* and *deviation*, stop for a minute and review the occupations listed above and see if you can visualize how flexion and/or deviation is a repetitive factor in their lives. Now review your own work, home and social activities, and identify the areas which either are or could be contributing to the development of a problem. Take some time to discuss this with colleagues and family and then, once you have a list, see what you can come up with to minimize the problem by altering your hand position where possible. If you're serious about understanding the problem, you'll make it a priority to do this, if not immediately, then in the very near future.

Before you take a few deep breaths and walk around or stretch, check out the position you've had your hands in while reading this book!

# Chapter 7
# Prevention – A Band-Aid Solution?

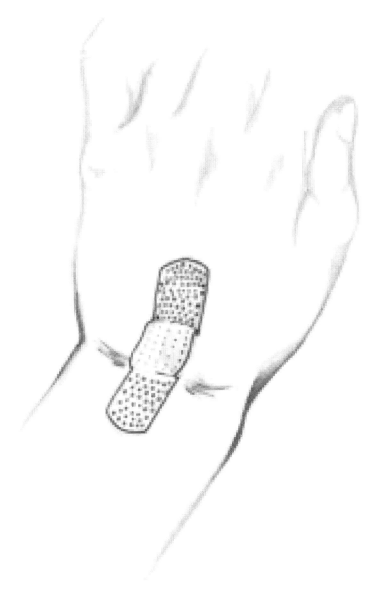

To this point I've told you how to identify the potentially harmful cumulative wrist postures and suggested you try to minimize the number of times you use these postures, but I haven't talked about *how* to minimize use of these postures. How are you going to remember to adjust your wrist and hand position where possible and still concentrate on performing your daily work and social activities?

One way, used by the ladies in the poultry plants, is to use an adhesive bandage, 4" to 6" long (Band-Aid, Elastoplast, etc.)! Put the bandage on the back of your wrist—about 2" on the back of your hand, stretching up your forearm to about 2" above your wrist. Each day, for a few days, put a fresh bandage, preferably the longer oblong shaped ones, on your wrist as shown in the diagram in this chapter. What will happen each time your wrist flexes or deviates? The bandage will pull on the skin of your wrist and get your attention. Now you know to change your hand position so that the bandage isn't pulling.

Make sure that the bandage you apply is hypo allergenic—you don't want any skin irritation to occur. For the very few of you who may get redness of the skin, stop using the bandage. You're going to have to concentrate on your hand position more than the rest of us, as you can't have the added advantage that the bandage gives. However, for the majority of you, you'll only need the bandage approach for about a week, by that time you'll have figured it out and made your adaptations. This was the only "tool" used by the workers in the previously mentioned Case Studies and that, combined with the workers' understanding of the problem, was enough in many cases to produce an effective reduction in their symptoms.

"How do I change my hand position and still do things safely?" That's a frequently asked question. My reply is usually, "You figure it out." I encourage you to take control by making your own adaptations and solving your own problems. What is known as "employee adaptations" is by far the most effective tool in combating these wrist problems. People are happier when they are given the chance to figure out solutions for themselves, rather than have some so called *expert* tell them how to change things. Management would do well to listen to these workers, as some of the recommendations are practical, cost effective, and often quite ingenious!

Remember, you don't have to avoid the positions completely, just be aware of their potentially harmful effects and minimize them as much as is practically possible.

Another problem to be aware of is compression of your wrist due to a tight watch strap, or tight fitting elasticized wrists on gloves. Obviously, these will compress the carpal tunnel and ultimately cause problems. If this affects you—stop doing it—starting today! It is that important and that simple.

Vibration to the wrist through use of tools is another area which can be helped by the use of ergonomics. An ergonomist can give advice on how your equipment can be modified to greatly ease the problem. You can also help by doing regular quick stretches to the muscles of your forearm as shown here:

Hold each stretch for about 30 seconds. Whichever one feels tight in your forearm is the one you need to work on. You will find a gradual decrease in pain and stiffness over a few days. Remember you have to stretch these muscles regularly to avoid the pitfalls of your occupation. Only if you "own" your problem can there be any real hope of resolution.

[note: if these stretches do not give relief, don't despair, get in touch with me and I'll explain how one treatment from someone who uses KCR as a treatment will almost definitely restore your wrists to normal and then the stretches will keep them that way. **yahugh@journeysend.ca**]

I hope this short chapter has given you the tools you will apply to take another step towards avoiding one of the pitfalls that can lead to the tragedy of being numbered among the *Early-Aging Work Force*.

## Chapter 8
# Don't Stick Your Neck Out!

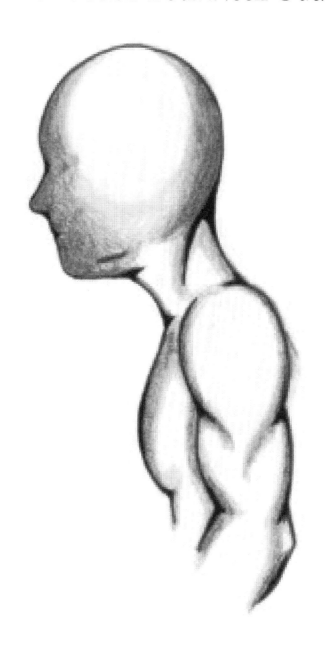

All you've been asked to do so far is to
1) breathe properly a few times a day,
2) stretch or walk about frequently during a day or evening spent sitting, and
3) watch your wrist position.

That's it! All the rest of the information has given you an understanding of why you should be doing this.

The final simple adjustment to your current lifestyle concerns a problem more epidemic than the other two combined. It is a problem which is impacting on millions of workers and their employers. And it is a problem not yet being recognized and/or addressed. It is one which is startlingly easy to remedy. I'm going to approach this by giving you several case histories and you'll come to understand the common link, then we'll talk about simple preventative techniques.

Case Study: A 45-year-old **Accountant/book keeper**.

Problem: numbness and tingling in his arms, neck pain, headaches, fear of losing his job as he had been forced to take time off work on two previous occasions due to his symptoms.

When he first talked to me, he threw down the gauntlet by aggressively stating, "Don't talk to me about computers and how they should be positioned because I don't use them! I work with ledgers all day and have to sit with my head forward. I know that's a lousy position for my neck, and I can't change it in work. So, when I get home I have my reclining chair in front of the television and I sit back for hours every night, *and I still have a lousy neck!*"

I simply said, "Hi, nice to meet you!" and extended my hand in greeting. Here was a man in constant pain and very afraid that he was rapidly becoming one of the *Early-Aging Work Force*. Medication, rest, and *postural adaptation at home* had not worked, and he was clearly becoming angry and desperate. Think about what he said, picture the activities mentioned, and you'll start to see what was going on.

The head forward posture at work could be helped with ergonomics and mini exercise breaks, but the real problem was that just like sitting, like the **Miners**, like the **Drywaller/Plasterer**, he had adapted to the posture of his neck and it actually *felt good*, despite the pain! Let's check out what he did when he went home—he sat back in the recliner and watched T.V. Your head is probably forward right now reading this book, which is similar to the position this man would be in working in ledgers at a desk. How far away is your chin from your chest? A couple of inches, maybe? Now, either sit back in your recliner or picture yourself doing so watching T.V. Can you see the screen while you're looking at the ceiling? Of course not. Your head is forward, supported by the cushioning of your chair and, note, how far away is your chin from your chest? A couple of inches, maybe? So how many hours a week was this man really in this position? Want to know something else? Once he realized that he had, in effect, created the same static position in his home environment, he said "You know, Hugh, I've just realized that I also sleep flat on my back each night with two pillows under my head!"

What chance did any treatment or rest have with making any lasting impact on this gentleman until he *figured it out*? None! By reducing his amount of time spent in this posture at home and at work, and realizing that the key muscles involved in his line of work had to be stretched regularly just like an athlete, this valued employee was working with no discomfort within four weeks. When I checked back with him six months later, he had had no recurrence of his symptoms!

Case Study: A crew of six outdoor workers in the **Oil and Gas Pipeline Industry.**

Average work experience: 12 years.

Problem: ongoing sick time due to neck and arm problems.

This was an experienced and valued group of workers. The company did not want to lose them or lay them off, but did not see any other future unless a solution could be found. It was obvious that due to the similarities in their symptoms, the problem had to be work-related. The organization had brought in specialists to give excellent back care programs, but the underlying feeling was that now, unfortunately, these men could no longer handle the rigors of their job and would ultimately have to be replaced.

It quickly became apparent to me that these men spent most of their long work day working with objects on the ground or below waist height. So, their chins weren't too far away from their chests most of the time, were they? Now came the real kicker! There is a lot of lifting in their job, and while their body mechanics for their backs while lifting was excellent, no one had discussed their neck posture while lifting. No one ever does, right? What has that to do with it anyway? Everything!

Visualize yourself lifting one end of a heavy table. Your feet are apart, your knees slightly bent, your back comfortably straight, your hands are under the edge of the table, and you're ready to lift. Are you looking down at the table? No, you're looking straight ahead, ready to lift. Picture how curved your neck is right now. As you lift, feel the muscles of your neck tighten, further compressing the curve. Is curving your neck like that is a good position? Might repeatedly compressing that curve cause problems over a period of time?

Absolutely.

The men on this crew quickly caught onto what I was trying to explain and started to give other examples of how their *postures* at work had been recurring in their other activities and actually *felt good*. They discussed how, when driving home tired at night, their chins would be poking further and further forward from their shoulders the more tired they got. Sound familiar? How many of us drive home like this? Check out how many other drivers do it too the next time you're stuck in rush hour traffic, and you'll start to grasp the picture. When these men got home, the recliner felt good (and we now know why). Some, when seated at a table, would put their elbows on the table and rest their chin on their hands! Not only were they damaging their necks while lifting, they had also adapted to this posture at work so that it actually felt normal and they were unconsciously repeating the postures throughout every component of their lives. Another sure fire recipe for pain and incapacitation! The next chapter will discuss how these postures can cause severe discomfort and disability and offer simple, effective remedies. For now, the important issue is one of awareness.

The work crew figured out the problem and implemented the changes with the result being that, six months later two had no symptoms, and three had only occasional minor discomfort. The sixth had not improved, but his x-rays had shown significant changes in his cervical spine due to the constant wear and tear on his joints. Prevention was a little too late to stop him from ultimately not being employed in this field of work. While this was unfortunate, it was good to know that five out of six workers had *turned it around*, and were no longer considered to be part of the *Early-Aging Work Force*.

How many workers, such as garbage collectors, warehouse workers, and various others, with similar job demands, can you think of? How wide spread is the problem now? Are you, or those close to you, in any of the categories mentioned yet?

Case Study: **Police Officer**—25 years of age.

Problem: Turned head to shoulder check while driving patrol car, initiating severe neck spasms—6 weeks off work. Back at work four weeks when, again while shoulder checking, spasms returned—8 weeks off work. Supervisors now questioning his ability to fulfill his duties on a regular and safe basis.

Traditionally, (rightly or wrongly) our city's finest are thought of in one of two categories. We envision them as either athletic and fit, or as "Captain Doughnut!" Right? Well, this officer was a fitness fanatic, and worked out seven days a week at the gym—hardly what we'd consider to be a high risk of injury. But it was the posture of his job, combined with his workouts which proved to be the cause of his ongoing problem.

First, while driving his patrol car, he spent most of the time with his chin forward to varying degrees (like the men in the work crew). What was going on at the gym? When we first go to workout, we are generally given a personal trainer to evaluate our current capabilities and set us up on a safe program, one targeted to our specific needs. The emphasis in lifting weights is usually on how to protect your back. For example, the usual instructions for doing bar bell curls are to place feet apart, have knees slightly bent, maintain your lumbar curve, and breathe out while lifting. The trainers even put you in front of a mirror so you can be constantly aware of proper technique. This is a highly commendable and recommended procedure, but there is a serious flaw here. How often are you instructed in watching your neck posture while lifting weights? Very few, if any of us, can answer yes to this one.

Picture yourself doing bar bell curls. What happens as you start to max out? As you strain to complete the curl, your chin starts to poke further and further forward, and your neck muscles get tighter and tighter. Correct? If you don't believe me, try it or go to the gym and simply observe others. As a physical therapist frequenting various fitness clubs over the years, I have often been asked for my business card from management because "We have a lot of bad necks in here, you know." But they never seem to realize why. Therefore the **Weightlifters** of the world are also unknowingly putting themselves at risk of chronic injury. The repeated curving and compressing of your cervical spine must eventually either directly cause or set you up for injury. The police officer's regular workouts combined with his *comfortable* habit of letting his chin stick forward while driving or sitting, created a gradual loss of range of motion, which couldn't take the requirements of quickly turning his head to shoulder check! Compare the officer lifting weights to the work crew lifting in the previous case study. It's the same problem. Once again, when the officer *figured out* his postural adaptation and implemented the changes outlined further on, his problem resolved. He returned to work, and a six month follow up showed he had had suffered no recurrence. (He was still working out strenuously seven days a week).

You can see how **truck drivers** and **delivery drivers**, who spend long hours behind the wheel and also load and unload their vehicles, fall into the same category.

Remember the worker who worked with ledgers all day with his head down towards his chest? Check out this next example.

Case study: **Cashiers in the Food Industry** yet again!

If you are thinking, "He's covered this one already!" you're right, I have, but we only talked about their wrists. Again, go back in your mind to waiting in the line up. Watch the cashier. No, not her wrists this time. Watch her head. What percentage of her time is her chin down towards her chest? Ninety percent of the time is a pretty fair estimate, correct? Oh boy, here we go again. Watch how when she looks up to talk to you, her chin is *poking* forward, with her neck curved. She hasn't got time to straighten right up to look you in the eye, and anyway it *feels good* the way she's doing it. Then she drives home, her neck is tired, and her chin is poking in her *comfortable* position. By *figuring it out* and making the necessary postural changes, I have seen dozens of these workers, male and female, eliminate their neck and wrist problems, enjoy job security and an overall higher quality of life because they now had minimal to no discomfort.

Case Study: **Power Line Workers/Linemen**

Problem: Every employee was suffering from neck problems!

These men spend most of their working time looking up! What position is their neck in constantly? Curved. What position becomes normal to them? Curved. So, how do they drive and sit? With their chins poking forward! They *figured out* the problem and workers taught workers. Awareness was the key. I hadn't thought of it until I had a particular patient who was a backhoe operator for a power line company, and he also had the same symptoms. However, these workers also spend a high percentage of their day looking up as they put the poles into position! The final numbers aren't in yet, but I know there is overall improvement and optimism in that work force.

Case Study: **Office Workers**.

I was asked to assess ten office workers in an insurance office for potential musculoskeletal problems. The company was totally unaware there could be any problems. The ten workers responded eagerly at the chance of discussing and solving their normal aches and pains. An amazing 67 problems with the potential of developing into disability were identified. With minimal treatment and emphasis on education and stretching, 64 of the problems were solved with 6 weeks and the workers had the knowledge to minimize the chances of recurrence.

We now know the effects of prolonged sitting can be detrimental. We also know these workers are at high risk of getting Carpal Tunnel Syndrome. We now know what they can do about it. But, how about the curved neck and the chin poking forward? It has been my experience that 98% of office workers have developed this as their *normal posture* throughout all of their daily activities. There are a huge number of these people, not only suffering from daily neck pain and headaches, but also the other ultimately disabling symptoms which will be discussed shortly.

Education and prevention programs are proving effective in getting a handle on these problems but, as before, the results only appear when the worker grasps understanding of how their bodies have adapted to their work environment and implement consistent changes.

Are you, or your family and friends included in this broad spectrum of indoor and outdoor workers who are at high risk of disability? I would bet that most of you are.

# Chapter 9
## So What's the Problem?

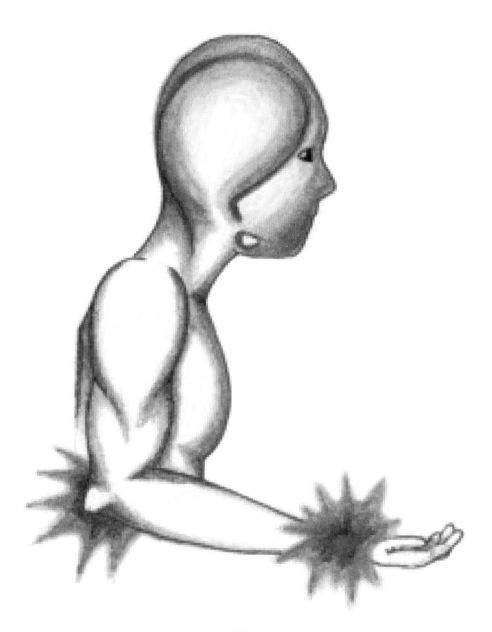

We've spent the last chapter demonstrating that many of us work, play and relax with our chins poking forward. How can this *comfortable, habitual* position contribute so much to the *Early-Aging Work Force*? I'll explain.

When you keep your chin poking up and forward, you increase the curvature in your neck, and compress the joints in your cervical spine. Over time, the muscles and tissues in the back of your neck shorten to accommodate this prolonged posture. This gradually restricts the range of motion in your neck. The results of this can be devastating! Tennis elbow, numbness and tingling in your arms, wrist pain, and weakness of grip can all be caused by the compression in your neck. Many workers have been tragically misdiagnosed as having tennis elbow or carpal tunnel syndrome, due to inadequate consideration of the influence of the neck. The frequent result for the workers is loss of employment, despite their doing everything they were told to do to resolve the problem.

How can my neck cause my elbow or hand to become disabled? It's not that difficult to figure out. How many of you either have had or know someone who has had sciatica? You know what I mean, when the pain is in your thigh or calf, and even in your foot. When someone says that their sciatica is acting up, we all know that their back is the problem even though the pain is in their leg and their actual back discomfort may be minimal. That's because that pressure on the sciatic nerve (where it exits the spine in your lower back) can cause symptoms at any or all points in its route down your leg. Therefore, compression of your lumbar spine, through prolonged poor posture or inflammation in this area through injury, can compress the nerves and give an array of symptoms in the areas these nerves supply. If you understand that, then when you realize that the nerves which leave the spine in the area of your neck supply your arms, just as the nerves which leave your lumbar spine supply your legs, it's very easy to see how many arm and hand symptoms develop due to compression of your neck! Not that difficult is it? It never ceases to amaze me how many medical professionals refuse to consider this, despite the fact that their patient's symptoms are not resolving with localized treatment!

I have seen many tennis elbows treated and recurring again and again, resulting ultimately, in loss of employment for the individual. Let's look at how compression in your neck can cause tennis elbow. Two long, stick like bones join your elbow to your wrist. These are known as the radius and ulna. Which is which? Turn your hand palm up and look at your forearm. The radius runs from your elbow, down the outside of your arm, to your wrist below your thumb. The ulna runs down the inside of your arm, from your elbow to your wrist below your little finger. These two bones are joined all the way up and down by a muscle called pronator teres. The job this muscle does when tightening up is to pull one bone over the other and help allow you to turn your hand palm down. The nerve supply to that muscle comes from between the bones of the lower neck and makes its way through the shoulder and down the arm to pronator teres. When this nerve is irritated at the neck, the signals it sends out causes the pronator teres to tighten up. This pulls the radius up into your elbow joint, causing compression, irritation, and inflammation of your elbow, resulting in the diagnosis *tennis elbow*.

Just as treating a leg won't make sciatica go away, treating an elbow frequently fails to resolve the problem because the cause, the neck, isn't being given any attention and probably doesn't hurt too much, apart from occasional stiffness. See how disability can develop?

Next on the list of problems created by the "poking chin syndrome" is pain between your shoulder blades. How can constantly "sticking your neck out" cause problems way down there? Easily! There are two large wing- shaped muscles in your neck and upper back called trapezius, or "traps" for short. They are situated one on each side of your spine, and run all the way down from the base of your skull to a level just below your shoulder blades. From the bottom they fan out and upward to your shoulder, and from there back up and into the base of your skull. If you picture a traditional kite, you'll have almost the exact shape, with each *trap* representing half of the kite.

So, if I keep my head forward and the upper part of my muscles shorten and adapt to this posture, surely it is going to pull on and restrict the lower part, ultimately creating problems. Make sense?

The next area seldom addressed as being caused by prolonged use of chin out posture is shoulder problems. When the muscles and connective tissue have adapted to sticking the neck out, they are no longer as elastic as they should be. Therefore, they start to restrict shoulder movement, and again an injury is just waiting to happen. Of particular note, are the muscles at the front on the neck which, when shortened, restrict the movement of the collar bone. A collar bone has to be able to *spin* upwards and downwards when you raise an arm forward and up over the head, or when you put your arm behind your back. It pivots with the shoulder where it joins at the part furthest away from your breastbone.

Feel along your collarbone, working towards your shoulder, and you'll feel where it sort of disappears into your shoulder. This junction is known as the AC joint. So, it's simple to figure how, if muscles responsible for assisting in the collarbone movement are not functioning properly and we keep trying to force our shoulders through movements that are becoming more and more difficult, it's a matter of time until injury results. Then, when and if the injury heals, we return to the same *feels good* posture and continue with our daily activities as before. And guess what? Here we go again! Entry into the *Early-Aging Work Force* on the horizon? It's an absolute certainty!

There is one other consequence of "sticking your neck out." This is the least understood and treated, but again is easily remedied and largely preventable. When we repeatedly overload our neck and shoulders, from repetitive tasks at work, or simply from our heads being forward all the time, or more commonly, a combination of both, damage occurs not only to the muscles and ligaments, but also to the nerves, which as you now know, supply your arms. What in effect happens is that the covering of each nerve, known as a sheath, when continuously stretched, suffers from an ever increasing amount of small tears in the lining. These are known as micro tears. When any tissue heals, it heals by scarring. This scar tissue adheres to everything around it (this is known as neural adhesion) and consequently further restricts the nerve, with the resulting random combination of symptoms described earlier, with the same catastrophic results.

Now that you understand the pitfalls of consistently sticking your neck out, the next chapter will tell you how to avoid them.

# Chapter 10

# To Find the Answer,
# Go Back to the Beginning

A good friend once reminded me, "Hugh, sometimes you have to go back to your roots to figure out where you're going," and how true that is for all of us. Yet just how true this is with the problem we have been discussing, did not hit me despite years of work on prevention, until I was in the middle of an inservice to postal workers. I was literally dumfounded at the simplicity of it, and it took me a couple of minutes to control my thoughts and excitement before continuing.

Here it is. As you know, workers from all walks of life have the problem of "sticking their neck out" so it clearly isn't an adaptation restricted to one particular industry. Remember how we recognized sitting as being alien to our bodies, but being accepted as normal because it feels good? Remember how some workers develop symptoms, having adapted to their occupations in a short period of time?

What job did we all have, at least between the ages of six and sixteen? That's right, school! Remember how you sat, how you wrote, how you looked up from your notes to see the teacher or the black board? There it is! The root of the whole thing! We adapted to this chin up position as "normal" and "feels good," probably before we were nine years of age!

Recently, I was invited to a local **schoolchildren** to discuss posture with students. A total of 34 students were present. They were all 14 to 15 years old, most likely bound for a career in the trades. During our routine *self checks*, which will be reviewed later, I was amazed to find that all of them had pronounced *poking chin*, but was stunned to find that only one out of the 34 had full range of motion in his neck! The very adaptation that is causing so many problems in later years is already strongly entrenched by the early teen years! Thanks to the teacher, Mr. Clyde Moore, for his foresight in allowing me access to his students and to instruct them in some preventative stretches. One young man jokingly said "I'll sue the school. They should have been warning me about this and doing something to help me prevent it." Interesting thought.

This short chapter may be the most important. The concepts offered in this book must be taken seriously by educators because only then can we practice true prevention and protect upcoming generations from the problems we now face and minimize their risk of joining the *Early-Aging Work Force*.

# Chapter 11

# A Little Chin Tuck

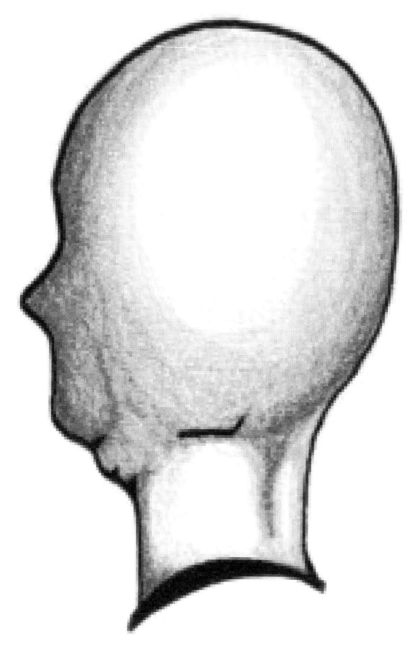

Sticking out your chin has become normal and "feels good." Most of you aren't aware that you do it. So, try a little test to find out. Read the following instructions carefully and then give it a try:

1) Sit up straight (straighten your back).
2) Look up from this book and fix your eyes on an object directly in front of you, at eye level.
3) Without tilting your head up or down, draw your chin slowly back towards your neck to give you the effect of a double chin.
4) Draw back as far as you can. (How much pressure to exert? The answer is "as far as you can." The only way to gradually increase the spine's flexibility is to go to the limit every time.)
5) Maintain that position, and swallow! Now let your head and neck relax again.


For those of you who do not have a postural maladaptation (and there are very few of you out there), this exercise will be easy and cause no discomfort. For the rest of you, the response can vary from "That was hard." to "That hurts." to "I can't do it!"

Now review the instructions again, carefully because they have to be done exactly, particularly numbers 3, 4, and 5. Practice it now five or six times, and each time you do it, feel what is happening in your neck.

Okay, done that? Relax, and by the way, congratulations! You've just learned the prime secret in preventing your neck from slowly, but surely moving you towards entry into the *Early-Aging Work Force*.

The bookkeeper/ accountant with the chronic neck, the work crew in the pipeline industry, the police officer, the weight lifter, the cashiers in the food industry, the power line workers, the office workers, and the school children we discussed earlier, all had varying degrees of the same problem. They were all able to reverse the problem, first by understanding it and secondly, by exercise!

What is the magic exercise? You just learned it! Try it a few times more before you read on. Remember, feel what is happening while you do it.

This exercise is not an instant fix. What you are doing is returning the neck gradually to a more normal posture. Only by habitually performing the exercise will you achieve and sustain results. This exercise is a major step towards:

1) Returning the joints in your neck towards a more normal alignment
2) by stretching the muscles and tissues all around your neck and across your shoulders
3) by stretching those stuck down nerves (remember the adhesions)
4) by reducing the compression on the blood vessels in your neck and shoulders, thus allowing better circulation
5) by retraining your brain into accepting this position as the "feel good" position
6) by moving quickly away from a major pitfall of the *Early-Aging Work Force*

That's a lot of good stuff happening, isn't it? Next, let's deal with some of the excuses I hear for not doing this exercise.

Excuse #1: "It gives me a double chin."

This is true, in most cases, it does! When you draw your chin back, the muscles running up the front of your neck probably sag and give the appearance of a double, or even triple chin. The double chin will go away in a few short weeks—if you persist with the exercise. Of course, if you are really overweight all over your body, then the double chin won't disappear completely—correct diet and exercise can take care of that for most people. I've had patients tell me that they've always had a double chin—it's the only place on their body that's fat! They inherited it from their grandma! It's almost laughable to consider that a person, especially someone thin as a rake everywhere else, can be fat in only one - three to six inch area of their body, but lacking any other explanation, what else could such a person think? Not knowing about postural maladaptations, they assume the double chins must be genetic.

How does continually sticking your chin out give you a double chin? It's very simple. Think of all the muscles in the front of your neck as a sheet of elastic running up from your collarbones and the top of your breastbone to the point of your chin. When you stick your chin out and keep it there, you stretch that sheet of elastic. So what happens when it has been constantly stretched, and then you tuck your chin in, as in our exercise? You shorten the distance between the point of your chin and your collarbones and breastbone, so the over-stretched sheet of elastic will sag. There's your double or triple chin looking back at you in the mirror!

Many patients are thankful to understand the cause of their double chins, but they still don't want one, thank you very much! Even though they understand the benefits, they're not interested in the exercise, because they don't think the cosmetic embarrassment is worth the potential health benefits. I understand how they feel, but they are missing one piece of information. That's why step #5 in the exercise is so important: to swallow when your chin is tucked back! The swallow forces the muscles in the front of your neck to contract and, as with any other muscle group, to tone up these muscles from flabby to trim and taut, you've got to exercise them regularly. So, another benefit of this simple exercise: lose your double chin! As I said in the opening chapter, try the methods I'm showing you, and keep trying for a while. The results will be rapid and clear, but you've got to be consistent about trying them. What have you got to lose? Have the implications of the phrase *Early-Aging Work Force* sunk in yet?

> Excuse #2: "I've been doing it regularly and all
> I'm getting is a really sore neck and headaches"

That's a pretty valid reason to quit, I agree! When some people start to move into a correct posture, they uncover something else going on in their neck and shoulders. On the positive side, these workers are finally listening to their body and are identifying their problems. On the negative side, they are saying "I won't do that exercise because when I do, it hurts." That's not curing anything, is it? It's simply avoiding the problem, and sooner or later it will catch up to them in the form of pain, injury, and possible disability.

If, after four or five days of trying the exercise, you still fall into this category, you should be seeing a competent health professional (more about them later) and have the problem identified and treated. The problem is often found to be some specific neural adhesions, discussed earlier, which are preventing you from doing the exercise correctly. These are easily corrected within a short space of time with treatment and more specific stretches. So don't quit the exercise if it starts to cause problems. Identify those problems and seek professional advice as to their cure. If you don't act on what your body is telling you, no one else will. I encourage that small percentage of you who fall into this category to seek the help you need to solve the problem.

For most people, an extreme reaction will not be a problem, and within a few weeks your daily aches and pains will feel greatly eased. There are some other stretches which you may want to consider, which I'll discuss in a later chapter. Without this Anchor Exercise, the chin tuck, all other exercises are doomed to failure. Make this one a part of your daily routine—starting now!

Excuse #3: "I keep forgetting to do the exercise—I'm too busy."

Some people can get really discouraged when I tell them I would like them to do this exercise 1000 times each day, which in a sixteen-hour day of activities, amounts to once every minute!

A little bit of simple biofeedback will solve the problem! Use the "Red Dot System." If you work in an office, or know someone who does, you have access to those little round adhesive red dots, usually used for marking file folders. Beg some of those. Or buy some at the stationers. Put them up where you'll see them. Put one on the rearview mirror of your car or truck. Every time you look in the mirror, you'll see the red dot and be reminded to do the exercise. You don't have to stop driving or concentrating, you just do it! If you watch T.V. at night, put a red dot in the corner of the screen. I've found it more effective for men to put this dot on their VCR, as it seems that we are constantly checking the time to see when we can play with the channel changer again! Put one on your bathroom mirror. One next to your oven, and one on your kitchen taps. One on the wristband of your watch! If you work at a computer or cash register, put one on the computer screen or tray. Now for the time and effort of putting up six or seven small red dots, you will have given yourself a pretty good biofeedback system. And you haven't had to give up any activities or drastically alter your lifestyle in any way.

One patient protested, "One thousand per day! I'll get nothing else done." The point is it has to become a habit to sustain the required postures. That's why the red dots are an excellent biofeedback tool. Eventually—in a matter of days—you will do it automatically, as with practice, it now "feels good." The average person swallows approximately every 30 seconds; that equals 1,920 times in a 16 hour day. If you accomplish half of these successfully, you will have succeeded. You may want to review Excuse #3 when you say you can't do 1,000 per day.

Excuse #4: "I keep forgetting to get myself some of those red dots!"

There is no excuse for this excuse! Patients are, in effect telling me that they understand what I've told them, they understand the benefits, but they don't consider the benefits a big enough priority to get a regime of doing the exercise underway. These are usually the same people who constantly complain their symptoms are not disappearing, they aren't getting better! They expect the system to fix them without their help. That's what gets most of us into chronic health problems in the first place.

I've come to a point where I won't waste my time on patients who refuse to help themselves, so I tell them that I won't see them again until they're implementing the red dot system. Most come back within a few days, finally owning their problem and making an effort to help solve it.

Case Study: **Postal Workers**

A couple of years ago, I was hired to teach these prevention exercises to the day shift workers at the main plant in a major city. This was a tough assignment. It was during a time of contract negotiations, and tensions and mistrust between union and management were at a high pitch. Some of the workers felt that they were being asked to work at a more than steady pace and were caught in a Catch 22 situation. If they didn't keep up, then automation and ultimate layoffs were just around the corner. Management was trying to produce a more cost effective and efficient organization, and felt that every move they made was being blocked by the labor movement. It hardly seemed the ideal scenario for me to obtain cooperation, as morale wasn't exactly at a peak in this work place. The workers had seen other inservices on health care come and go, without any lasting impact on their well being, and some of them viewed this latest program as some form of management plot to undermine their job security.

This was not the case for all the employees. A caring and overworked occupational health group persisted in the program's organization. The open- mindedness of most employees to give me a chance, allowed me access to this dedicated and often misunderstood group of men and women. I talked to them in small groups of around fifteen at a time, until I had met with close to three hundred workers. As I stated earlier, our work force, the life blood of our economy, are not stupid people. Their questions were direct and blunt, and I learned a lot from them. At the end of the day, they realized that all I was asking of them, if what I said made sense to them, was to try it.

Two weeks later I called the plant to see how things were going and was delighted to hear that *red dots* had sprung up all over the place and that workers were reminding each other (using various forms of humor) to keep tucking their chin in and swallowing. After six weeks, I had a follow up survey distributed to the workers who had participated. The survey asked for comments, and I encouraged honesty so I could rate the effectiveness of what they had done. The workers were not to sign the survey sheets, so anonymity was guaranteed, and, the sheets were to be returned to me directly and not to be scrutinized by management. The results showed that 82% of the work force were pleased with themselves for persisting with the exercise, and stated a noticeable decrease in their daily aches and pains. When the workers took control of the problem, the result was a huge decrease in discomfort with consequent increase in personal and group morale. To this great group of people, I offer my respect and thanks.

We've identified a huge postural problem here, haven't we? So what are you going to do about it? Give it a try. Get your red dots up, do the exercise while you're reading this book, and when you start to feel the benefits, teach your family and colleagues how and why to do it.

People teaching people, worker teaching worker will increase knowledge and understanding for each and every one of us. Be a part of it and let it begin for you right here and now!

## Chapter 12

# Just Grit Your Teeth and
# Keep Going . . . and Going . . .
# and Going!

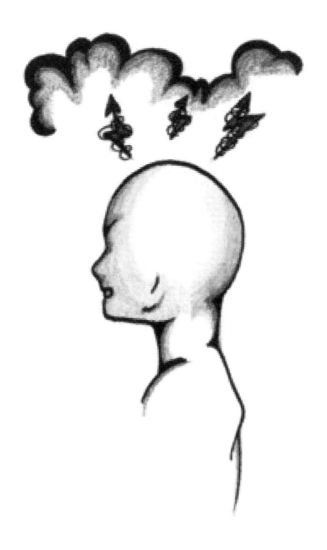

To briefly review again what we've covered so far, all I've asked you to do is

1) Breathe properly, regularly,
2) Watch your wrist posture (if it's applicable to you),
3) Tuck your chin in and swallow regularly.


That's it! Nothing you can't handle. I hope I've also given you a better understanding of how postural adaptations to the work place affect you and those you care about.

This next topic I'm sure you'll find it interesting and in many cases, relevant to you or someone close to you. It is teeth clenching and the problems it creates. It is only right at this point that I thank a man, an eminent physician by the name of Dr. Rocobado, for helping me understand the ramifications of this repetitive action. He has given a series of international lectures on the topic. His work is well worth reading.

Most of us know that clenching our teeth can often be associated with stressful times. It is a common response in many animals (including man) who have a jaw!

Example A: You're walking down a dimly lit back alley. Suddenly, as if from out of nowhere, there is a medium -sized dog right in front of you! (Let's make it a black dog, always a wee bit more menacing, huh?). The dog has bared his teeth (clenched) and is making threatening growls towards you as you advance, although now, you're slowing significantly!

Despite the probable flutter of fear, or in some cases, full blown terror, in your heart, you know instinctively that there are only two choices open to you (presuming you haven't already had a heart attack). You know that, first, the dog could have a serious intent to harm you, in which case slowly backing up and leaving the area might be your best course of action. The second possibility is that the dog is bluffing and a straight forward aggressive action on your part will send him running for cover. No one ever had to explain it to you. You know it instinctively that the animal in front of you, clenching its teeth, is ready to fight or run. Now you have to decide which option is on the table, and act accordingly. I hope you make the right call!

Example B: You're working at your job and the phone is driving you crazy. Your boss is always calling about trivial stuff and you're getting further and further behind in your work. Frustrated, you grit your teeth and mutter under your breath, "If that phone rings one more time, I'll tear it out of the wall and . . ." RRRING! RRRING! You grab the phone and say sweetly, "Hi, this is (your name) speaking. How can I help you?" You deal politely with the call, slam the phone back down, and return to gritting your teeth and muttering profanities when, guess what . . . the phone rings!

Somehow you survive the day. Neck and shoulders hurting, head pounding, you swear at every other driver and traffic light on the way home, snarl at your family, and go to bed totally exhausted. You hope that tomorrow is a better day, which if you're lucky, it will be. So, how did you get through your crisis? You gritted your teeth and kept on going!

Example C: We all have a memory of our childhood when we ran from something, real or imaginary (down that hallway or past that door, or across that yard), and we were so scared it felt as though our feet were barely touching the ground. Remember how tightly our teeth were clenched? We were ready to fight or flee, and in this case flight was the chosen option, and our body responded accordingly. Didn't it?

Teeth clenching is one potentially lifesaving response to any stressful stimuli, and when we clench our teeth, we trigger the sending of adrenalin into our system. This adrenalin helps the brain to go on alert, and the muscles to go on standby by increasing their tone and putting your whole body in a position to fight or flee just like the dog in the alley. It is a survival mechanism which has proved effective in allowing us to cope with threatening situations, and to survive as a species since the beginning of mankind.

76

How does that affect you and me today? I used to wonder why many of my patients with neck problems were so obviously tense or constantly tired. While I could usually alleviate their neck problems, they were frequently back within months, asking me to *fix* them again. They were just as tense and tired as before, and while the repeat business was always welcome, I couldn't figure out why the effects of treatment were not longer lasting. There was obviously something missing. Dr. Rocobado's teachings gave me the missing piece in the puzzle.

When you constantly clench or grind your teeth, you are in effect, consistently triggering the fight or flight reflex. One effect is that you probably don't have anything close to a restful sleep at night. Your brain tells you all the things you "have to do tomorrow, should have done today, should have done twenty years ago, will have to do twenty years from now, better get up and do it now." Because the fight or flight has been triggered, the brain is trying to identify the threat and search its memory banks in an effort to deal with the "unseen enemy." The brain is constantly saying "Go, go, go!" The muscles of your arms and legs have become chronically fatigued from the constant standby mode. While the brain is saying "Go!" the arms and legs are saying "Get outta here—we died six months ago!"

"Just give me a needle to put me to sleep for about two weeks and I'll be just fine," is a common plea of these patients. They're exhausted! What also happens as they fatigue more and more is, they clench their teeth and say to themselves, "Come on, you can do it, get moving!" The vicious circle of stress and fatigue continues. Stress tolerance quickly diminishes. Things that wouldn't have upset them a few years ago sure trigger upsets now!

Those close to you, at home and at work, don't understand what's happening, so they begin to withdraw from you. You also don't understand what's happening, so you blame them and clench your teeth while sending yourself the message, "Who needs them anyway?" The ongoing effects in the work and family environment can be devastating and often, apparently irreparable.

What would be the ongoing effect of your muscles always being tense and fatigued? Would you possibly be more prone to injury than the average person? Would you take longer to recover from injury than the average person? Would you have a higher chance of recurring injury that the average person? You know it!!

So, there it was, the missing piece in the puzzle. What can be done about it? First, if you suffer from the pattern outlined in this chapter, you can realize that you're not a "burn out," you're not "losing it," and you're not just "too old to handle things the way you used to." Realize that what has happened is a perfectly normal bodily response to consistently clenching your teeth, and it can be altered. A trip to your physician and orthodontist may well be indicated to check for physical dysfunction of your jaw, and implementation of corrective measures. However, you can start decreasing the number of times you start clenching your teeth right now!

How? When you do your "chin tuck and swallow" exercise, do it with your teeth slightly apart! At least that'll be 1,000 times a day you're not clenching. That, in itself, along with understanding of the problem is often all it takes to start making a noticeable improvement in your well being. Try it. You'll know it's working when you suddenly not only feel exhausted, but start sleeping so deeply that you have difficulty awakening in the mornings. Don't panic, and don't fight it!

All that is happening is that your body is finally starting to relax and grabs at every chance to replenish the energy lost over the years. You're getting better! This spell appears to last anywhere from a few days to a few weeks, and you start waking up refreshed and ready to start your day (as long as you keep doing your exercise). Whatever aches and pains you are being treated for, you now have a real chance of resolving for the first time.

Some patients say to me, "What's the point? I still grind my teeth at night."

My reply is "Yes, you will grind at night for a while, but while you haven't eliminated the problem, and that may take professional help, you have greatly reduced the problem."

There is another group of patients who do not respond to orthodontic splints and frequently bite right through them, despite excellent orthodontic assessment. We'll discuss what may be their problem in the next chapter. For most of you, you know the problem, and you now know the possible solution, so get to it and see what happens!

# Chapter 13
# Stress Out – Burn Out

Over the years, through careful observation and with the teaching and assistance of some highly recognized mentors, I have become fairly adept at identifying and working with stress disorders. It is now widely recognized that people who are stressed and tense are not only more prone to the types of injuries I see on a daily basis, but are also slower to recover from injury, as well as having a much higher risk of recurrence than the more relaxed individual. Therefore, I had to start paying more attention to this component if I wanted them to achieve resolution of their physical problems. It was only when I recognized how many people were constantly stressed and didn't know it, that I came to realize that I too was in that category and some changes had to be made in my own approach to life.

Allow me to clarify that stress is normal is our lives. It is the amount and type of stress that affects function.

Positive stress (Eustress) has a beneficial influence on muscle tone. Negative stress (Distress) has a detrimental effect on muscle tone. Therefore, while the positive stress of the fight or flight reflex may greatly increase our chances of survival when threatened, the negative stress of continually creating that state of fight or flight by excessive teeth clenching has a detrimental effect on our well being.

From the previous chapter you now understand how teeth clenching contributes towards accumulated stress and you know what to do about it. The key is understanding the process. As I said, I am not a psychologist, nor do I pretend to practice psychology—that should only be done by qualified professionals. My message in the last chapter and this one, is that before you can get help, you have to recognize and admit that there is a problem! I'm not saying that we all have to go see a psychologist or a psychiatrist. I am saying we should recognize "burn out" and take steps to prevent it as it will probably shorten your life and certainly can propel you into the *Early-Aging Work Force*.

Case Study: When I was coaching university sports, I had the pleasure of working with Dr. Cal Botteril, an eminent Olympic Sports

Psychologist. While I learned many excellent, effective techniques to enhance team performance, I asked for his opinion on one of my players, and what I discovered in this process has a direct relationship to many of you!

Here was a young player, intelligent, fit, a great athlete and leader, one I was trying to build my team around. In preparation for conference play in the fall, we trained and played tournaments all summer. This young man's drive, skill, and leadership was a huge motivational factor to the other players.

The semester started and we moved into our scheduled games. For three years I watched this lad change from the leader, into an almost non-involved participant, which not only affected his performance, but quickly sent team moral for a loop. I knew it wasn't because he didn't care, he loved the game and had a strong desire to win. I couldn't get to the bottom of it and relations between us were frequently strained, as I expected so much more of him than he was giving.

So, I asked Dr. Botteril's opinion, and he asked this young man if he could work with him. The young athlete readily agreed. A short time later, both the player and I had the answer we were looking for. What was happening was that this man did indeed want to excel at everything he did, so while we played over the summer, he had no other distractions from sport and did excel. However, once classes started, he also wanted to excel there, and took five full courses each semester. He got up each day ready to beat everybody at everything, but by the time he got to my practices in the evening, he had nothing left, mentally, to give, and his physical performance was the first place it showed! By the time he got to me, he was burnt out and, over time this reflected not only on his sport, but on all of his activities, to the extent that it appeared he was underachieving.

It was this young man's last season playing with our team before graduating, so I never got to see how he changed in that respect, but I do know that he did get his degree and move on in his chosen career. This fit, healthy, and motivated man, had been burning out and didn't realize it. Hopefully, the most important thing he learned at university was the life lesson taught to him by Dr. Botteril, who showed him how to reduce his stress and gave him some techniques for use throughout the rest of his life. If he took the lessons to heart, I am sure that he will realize his full potential and be an outstanding success at everything he goes for in life.

How might this apply to you? You're not a high performance athlete, and you're not attending university, so what's my point? How many of you are totally exhausted at the end of the work day, and arrive home to your family with nothing left to give? (Just as the athlete had nothing left to give.) How many of you are too busy to relax and do the things you'd like to do? How many of you have forgotten what the things you liked to do are, as you're so busy with other "highly organized activities?" How many of you are working long hours (often unpaid, but expected of you) to keep the work place afloat? How many of you fit all of the above? How many others of you are saying to yourselves right now, that's how your life is but you can't do anything about it?

Well you can do something about it and, in fact, you are now! You're reading this book, aren't you? That means you have already learned some techniques for stress reduction and, hopefully, are applying them at this time. If not, stop reading, take a few deep breaths, stand up and stretch, and do a few "chin tucks" while you're at it. Feel better? Then on we go.

Many pro active industries have recognized the impact of stress on their work force and have offered in-house availability of counseling for stress reduction. While that is a huge step in the right direction, the problem I am seeing is that their bosses and colleagues are the last people those in trouble want to know that they are burning out. Therefore, the last place they would ever admit to having a problem is in the work place. They don't want to give the impression that they can't cope, and think that first it would be an admission of weakness to seek help, and secondly, are afraid that if management feels that they have a problem in dealing with the work load, they will ultimately be replaced and become part of the *Early-Aging Work Force*. Consequently, they continue with their silent struggle, until they no longer are able to cope, and ultimately suffer disability and loss of employment, not to mention potential loss of home and family due to marital breakdown!

The point is, recognition of the problem is the first step for each of us. The next step, just as with the postural adaptations, is ownership and taking control of the problem before it overcomes you. Then, and only then, can we have any hope of winning. The system is currently unable to fix these things for us. We have to accept the responsibility and make the effort to change. In other words, now that you understand the problems, you have to accept the responsibility for changing them, and realize that you are now accountable for making the changes necessary in your daily life. If the work force can do this and show management they are making a worthwhile contribution to decreasing disability rates, then the pressure *really* moves to the corporate level to do their part in return.

Some of you are now thinking that your employer doesn't care and wouldn't spend a dime to help you no matter what you did. That is a tragic, but often true, scenario which we'll look at a little later on, but if what you say is true, then the only person who can help you—is you! If your boss doesn't care if you join the *Early-Aging Work Force*, then you have to care, and at least *you now have the tools and understanding* to fight back and really make a difference, if you'll just persist.

What techniques work for me? The breathing and the stretches I've shown you sure help. Realizing that I have to balance my time between work and relaxation, and then doing something about it, has made a tremendous difference. This is one which I work hard at, hopefully every day. It sounded strange to me the first time I was told I had to work hard at relaxing, until I realized that I was working hard at everything else except relaxing. At that time in my life, what I thought was relaxing was actually exhaustion, namely, hitting the couch with the channel changer every night. I was burning out and didn't know what to do about it. I was too busy to relax and didn't have time to add another task—work or relaxing—to my schedule. In other words, relaxing just wasn't a priority. I was running my engine flat out, but wouldn't even stop for fuel, far less a tune up! I was in too big a hurry to do anything about it. It's a recipe for disaster, isn't it?

I still have to make a conscious daily effort to make myself a priority in my life, but the benefits are huge. When I start to slide into my old ways, thankfully, my partner, Jane, can see the signs and makes me pay attention to the important things again. We each have to make our own effort to balance our lives, and different things will stimulate different people. For me, some of the best and most practical information I have learned was from a book called *The Monk Who Sold His Ferrari* by Robin S. Sharma. The title initially got my attention, but the content certainly had a huge impact on giving me some daily goals, and the means of achieving them. Robin, if you ever read this book, thank you for sharing your insights, and hopefully, "my cup is still empty!" Taking the time to plan my activities has worked wonders for me too, and by persisting in use of my Franklin Quest Journal, which is an excellent way of organizing my work load and goals, there is definite order developing in the often chaos of my life.

These strategies might not work for everyone, but, having recognized the problem, you can now do something about it. It's up to you, for as I said, if you don't do something about it, no one else will. Good luck to you all.

[**note**: In the years since I wrote this book I have become aware of other factors involved in stress and have worked successfully with many levels of patients suffering from PTSD. Further I have also been highly successful in working with stress reduction in Children labeled as in the Autism Spectrum and with their families. For more specifics please contact me personally at **yahugh@journeysend.ca**]

# Chapter 14
## The Long and the Short of It

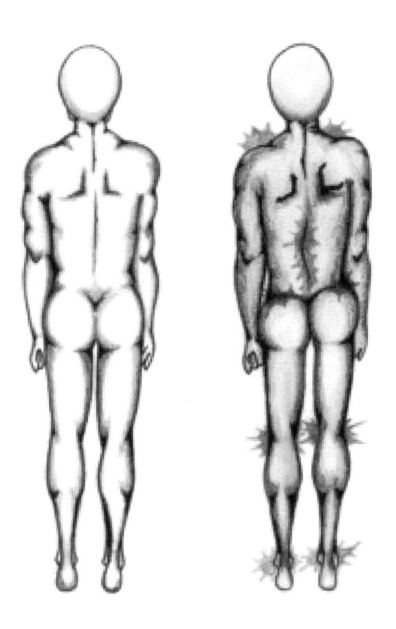

**Leg Length Difference! As of October 2013 there are over 39 Million articles on this on the Internet!** This is probably the chapter that I'll need your help with the most! It's easy to visually demonstrate, but much more difficult to put down on paper, so I really need your help to picture each step I talk about. This problem creates the least understood and most misdiagnosed set of symptoms I ever see, and I see it every day! Here is a list of just a few of the symptoms/diagnoses that my patients present with this condition. (They may have one only or they may have them all!) Weak Ankles; Tight Calf Muscles of Hamstrings; Chronic Knee Pain; Dislocating Knee Caps; Chronic Hip Pain; recurring Groin Injury; Chronic Low Back Pain; Chronic Pain between their Shoulder Blades; Shoulder Pain; Chronic Neck Pain; Arthritis; Pelvic Problems; Fibromyalgia; Chronic Fatigue Syndrome; teeth clenching; jaw problems;

If there is no obvious cause to the particular problem the worker has then it's very possible that he or she has one leg longer than the other! Some medical professionals feel that

1) everybody has one leg longer than the other, and

2) if it's only 1/2" it's not important.


It has been my experience that any difference is VERY important and I have proved it over and over again. It really frustrates me when I see workers who have lost their job and their quality of life through chronic conditions which have been essentially been caused by a leg length difference, especially when I know that the problems were probably completely preventable!

This is not rocket science, it's common sense, as I hope you will come to understand. When you grasp it, you can discuss it with your health care professional and demand proper treatment, which is why I'm writing this book.

I, like many of my colleagues, have taken many ongoing post-graduate courses in physical therapy or specific areas like the spine, pelvis, knee, and ankle, but I never really started to put it all together until 1982. At that time I had a discussion with, to my mind, the best physical therapist I have ever known. I am referring to Mr. Erl Pettman, for the last twenty years, a leading light in physiotherapy and currently practicing in Abbotsford, British Columbia, that is when he's not on the lecture circuit. Here is the example that really started to put it together for me.

Case Study: University athlete with undiagnosed constant ankle pain.

One of the players trying out for my squad was a young man whom I had coached a couple of times in the youth program in previous years. He had always shown a potential to be a real quality player, but I felt that he lacked a little self-confidence, and I was sure that would remedy itself with maturity. This young man graduated well from high school, was accepted for university, and came to try out for the soccer squad. When we were eventually down to about 30 players trying out for a final 16 spots, competition was intense and often physical. Initially I was confident this young man would make the squad, but by the end of the first week, he appeared timid when going into tackles, and overall was not showing the speed I knew he was capable of. Finally, I took him aside and asked him what was wrong. He told me he had a painful foot. I examined him, and, apart from a little stiffness of mobility, could find no obvious inflammation or injury. I began to suspect that the lack of confidence and consequent under achieving was again surfacing and, if so, he wouldn't survive the final selection cuts in our roster.

Just in case I was wrong and had missed something, I thought I'd call Erl, whom I had met through attending some of his courses. I phoned him over 500 miles away, and told him what was going on. With minimal hesitation he replied, "He's a mouth breather, isn't he?"

I couldn't believe what I was hearing and thought this man I had come to respect, was either hard of hearing or trying to be funny. Either way, it seemed to me I'd wasted my dime on the call. Then I calmed down a bit, thought about the athlete in question, and realized that indeed he was a mouth breather! While a highly intelligent lad, he always had that slack jawed, open mouthed, half awake expression on his face! How the heck did Erl know that and what the hell did it have to do with his ankle?

Erl explained that mouth breathers push their head forward more than the rest of us while running, and that shifts the overall weight of our body slightly further over the ankle joint, producing exactly the set of symptoms that my athlete was complaining of. I thanked him and hung up, still not by any means convinced, but willing to give it a try, as I could see no other avenue of hope in this case.

I asked the player to trust me and visit the dentist. He did. The problem was his incoming wisdom teeth, which the dentist removed within two days. Within a week, he was no longer walking around with his mouth hanging open, but more importantly, his ankle pain was gone. His speed had returned and he won a spot on our squad.

While I still wasn't too sure of what had happened, I realized that if removing his wisdom teeth had indeed been the answer to the ankle problem, I'd better start looking a lot closer at the whole structure of the body (known as the kinetic chain) with a lot of my other patients, if I wanted to obtain successful resolution of their symptoms!

By continually assessing for problems throughout the kinetic chain, I gradually became aware of the importance of the leg length difference and the restrictions it causes throughout the human body. It's easy to see what can happen to your body if one leg is longer than the other. All you have to do is stand up straight now, keeping your left foot flat on the floor, and your knees straight, raise your right heel off the floor a couple of inches or so (you can stay on tip toe on your right foot). What happens? Your body tips over towards the left because your pelvis now goes up to the right, doesn't it? You're not going to walk around, or even stand like that normally are you? Of course not, you're going to straighten up so you're not leaning to the side. So, go ahead, straighten up! (Don't put your heel down!) Notice how you've had to curve your lower back and then shift your shoulders to appear straight? Can you imagine the effects on your back and shoulders if you had to walk around like that, or play sports?

As I said, it's not rocket science, is it? While the effects of the adaptations due to a leg length difference are clear when you've just made one leg a couple of inches longer than the other, the cumulative stresses and strains on the joints and ligaments are just as devastating over time on the individual who only has 1/2" leg length difference, and the real problem then is one we've encountered many times already in this book. No one brought the danger to the worker's attention before, and he or she didn't know it was a problem because the overall posture felt good, didn't it?

It's now clear to you how having a leg length difference can affect your spine, so how many of you, or your children have been told you have scoliosis, and it's either genetic or just bad posture? Read on and you'll know what to do about it before the end of this chapter.

To continue, if I have a leg length difference, my spine is curving and bending all the way up to the base of my skull to accommodate, isn't it? Any wonder I get headaches? Any wonder I get jaw (TMJ) problems? (No you're probably thinking, "Oh no! Now he's saying that a leg length difference can give me a jaw problem? He's as off the wall as that Pettman guy!")

Stay with me and work it through. As the spine twists and turns to accommodate the leg length difference and the tilt in your pelvis, the changes in the position of the vertebrae continue right up to the top, where the 2$^{nd}$ cervical vertebrae rotates to the side. Remember, we do not normally walk with our head tilted. We will alter our gaze so it stays horizontal, if possible. This vertebrae is in close alignment with your jaw, so when the vertebrae moves, something has to give to accommodate it. Yep, you've got it, your jaw. And there my friends, is an example of how a leg length difference can give you TMJ problems!

These patients are often the ones who bite through their corrective mouth splints, because the jaw cannot be corrected until the neck is, the neck cannot be corrected until the back and pelvis are corrected and the leg length difference addressed and dealt with. Make sense? I hope so. (Possible cause of the teeth clenching we spoke of in the last chapter?)

Now, how many of you ladies never carry your purse on one particular shoulder because it keeps sliding off? I want to make it clear to you right now that it is NOT your fault. You can't help it. No one told you about the effects of a leg length difference before did they?

Don't feel overwhelmed by the problems at this point, because this one is usually fairly quick and easy to correct, often with astonishing results!

Later I'll discuss the knee and ankle problems but for now I want to explain what exactly causes a leg length difference and what can be done about it. Once identified, leg length difference, can be put into one of two categories. First there is a true leg length difference, and secondly there is an apparent leg length difference. How do you find out if someone has one leg longer than the other? Dead easy!

Have the person lie on his or her back on the floor, with no shoes on, and you kneel down at his or her feet. Now, put your thumbs just below the person's inside ankle bones. Your thumbs should be touching the lowest part of the person's ankles. Next, lean forward so you are looking directly down over their ankles. Is one thumb lower than the other? If it is, chances are you're looking at a leg length difference! It's that simple. Now you take them to see someone who will do something about it, and listen to your concerns.

What did I mean by a true leg length difference and an apparent leg length difference? A true leg length difference is where you have one leg naturally longer than the other. This can be easily identified by your physician or other rehab specialist by using a measuring tape. If it's found you have a true leg length difference, then you probably need a raise or orthotic in the shoe of the shorter leg and the problem is solved!

If, however, it is found that you have an apparent leg length difference, you have a different, but still treatable, problem. The apparent difference is also easily identified by simple measurements. Of the patients I have seen with a leg length difference, only about 5% actually had a true difference. The other 95% classify as apparent.

How can someone have one leg which is apparently shorter than the other, but isn't? Once again, this is simple body mechanics. Follow through it with me now. The problem begins at the tail bone. Your tail bone is basically a big, thick upside down, triangle shaped bone that sits between your hips and buttocks, with your spine resting like a pillar on top of it, and your pelvis attached to the sides of it. Now, if you have had a fall on (or a blow such as a kick) to the tail bone, the impact can shift the tail bone from vertical, to an angle off center. So instead of looking like this, it now sits like this:

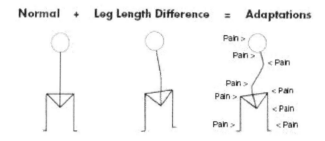

If I add the legs and feet to the tail bone, now guess what I see?

Remember earlier I asked you to stand and lift one heel up and note what happened to your spine? Well, here is the displacement again, only this time it's usually caused by trauma, and the muscles and ligaments have made a postural adaptation to altered body mechanics, and you don't even notice it anymore as it now feels normal, with the result of the list of problems mentioned earlier. Some professionals also say that the whole problem of leg length difference can be caused from your neck not being aligned properly, and the chain reaction throughout your spine and ultimate shift in your pelvis is all from up there. This has not been my experience, but at least they are recognizing there is a problem with a leg length difference and that's the important thing.

How may of you have had ongoing problems and no one has ever checked you to see if one leg is longer than the other? Now you can have a friend check your ankles as I taught you, and find out! From there, find someone who will do something about it. It has been widely speculated that an apparent leg length difference can be corrected with postural reconstruction in about three months of rehabilitation. This is true and is effective for many. However, it is my experience that by using my own method of gentle postural correction known as Kinetic Chain Release (KCR) the apparent leg length difference is usually totally correctable in a much shorter time frame—usually 3 visits to my clinic!

The results achieved are easily sustainable in most cases, with dramatic return to activities and pain relief the norm.

So, when your health professional tells you that you have a leg length difference, ask them if it is true or apparent! If they don't know the difference, or say that there is no such thing, get out of there as fast as your long and short leg will carry you!

For those who were wondering:

How does this problem can cause knee and ankle problems?: When you have a leg length difference, and have both feet planted on the ground, the stresses going through those legs must be different because the center of gravity for the weight of your upper body is shifted. This means that one leg is carrying a bigger load than the other, with the weight coming down through the leg slightly off center, often resulting in a patient who has frequent ankle sprains and thinks that his or her ankles are just weak, or they crack lots, or who reports that they have a dislocating knee cap with no history of injury, "it just started to happen."

What is the effect of the altered weight bearing of apparent leg length difference have on the ankles? I have found that it causes moderate to severe restrictions in the bony joints of the ankles; particularly those around a central ankle bone known as the TALUS. This bone accepts forces from and transmits forces to your shin, your heel and the ball of your foot. As it becomes restricted, the potential restrictions are many. It also makes sense that, if not addressed, then every time we are standing or walking, the physical problems we have discussed, throughout the body, are enhanced.

Some therapists work towards correcting the spinal alignment, others also consider the pelvis and others work with the craniosacral component; but, if the base, in other words the ankles, are still restricted then the whole set of problems will just keep recurring, over and over again. So, for those who say that the neck is the problem I say "Heads or Talus?" It doesn't matter as long as you address the whole body. [**note:** any occupation classified as High Impact on the ankles knees and spines should pay particular attention here. Many people stop attending **High Impact Aerobic** classes despite totally loving the participation. This is neither their fault or the fault of the programme. It is the anomalies of the leg length difference which are already in place and get aggravated by repetitious high impact activity. Many have returned to full participation after following the steps of KCR (below).]

If you have ANY of the physical problems outlined earlier in this chapter and the possibility of a leg length difference has never been addressed and corrected, then you are edging closer and closer to joining the *Early-Aging Work Force*. So take control of your life and make sure you get this possibility investigated quickly and thoroughly! If you are having difficulty in finding assistance (or in some cases having difficulty being taken seriously by your physician/therapist et al.) then contact my organization at: **www.kineticchainrelease.com**

**Now for the good news! Despite 39 million articles mostly saying that leg length difference is not easily correctable, I have proven them wrong. My protocol Kinetic Chain Release can be learned by anyone and corrects most leg differences instantly with consistent "miraculous" results usually in one session of less than 30 minutes. This groundbreaking gentle protocol alone can return millions of workers and athletes to performance levels at work and at play. Find out for yourself on-line at www.kineticchainrelease.com and if you want to know more, feel free to contact me personally.**

## Chapter 15
# Check it Out

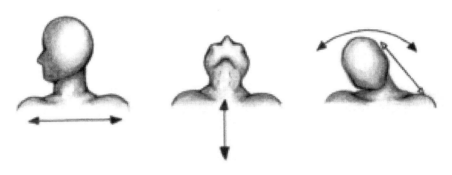

Whether you feel that you are in the best or worst shape of your life, a simple regular check of your own range of motion will usually identify areas that need a little more attention. It will confirm to you where your postural adaptations to your occupation or to previous injury have taken place.

Case Study: The **D.J. Disc Jockey** "Jock"

This was a classic example of how potential injury and disability can easily be identified. Six years ago I was teaching a prevention program at a fitness club and had the participants paired up to look at each other's range of motion and see what they could find.

One young man in attendance was not participating in the class. He was covering it for a story for his local radio program. However, to make up even numbers for this part of the demonstration, he gladly agreed to participate, confident that as a young, fit, and athletic individual, he'd find nothing of personal benefit to him in the topic of the *Early-Aging Work Force*. So it came as quite a shock to him to have his partner point out that he was extremely restricted in his range of motion when he turned his head to the right or when he tried to bring his right ear down towards his right shoulder! He did, however, immediately grasp the possible problems this might cause for him and eagerly got involved in the discussion as to what was going on.

While I talked to him, I noticed he sat listening intently and comfortably, and his head was tipped slightly to the left while he did so. The rest was easy! As I said, this man worked at a local radio station and spent a large portion of his day on the telephone interviewing local authorities and celebrities, gathering information for his show. He had been doing this for six years, talking for hours each day on the phone while working at his computer, with the phone tucked in between his left ear and his left shoulder so that he could use his hands. So, here he was, comfortably looking at me with his head almost in the same position! Postural adaptation to the job site again, isn't it? He'd been doing it for so long that his body had adapted to the position and he now spent most of his home and social time in that position because it felt good.

The adaptive shortening of his muscles on the left side of his neck were not only putting constant compression on the nerves and blood vessels in that area, but would no longer stretch enough to let him turn his head properly to the right! This 24-year-old athletic individual was not only a high risk of eventual injury, but also of becoming a prime candidate for the *Early-Aging Work Force*. However, having identified the problem, we implemented the chin tuck exercise, a couple of other more specific stretches to be done regularly, and got him to wear a headset instead of sticking the phone between his ear and his shoulder. The result was full range of motion within four weeks and the knowledge and understanding he had gained should last him a lifetime. Once again, the worker figured it out.

Check out your neck right now!

Slowly lower your chin until it is resting comfortably on your chest. No cheating! Keep your mouth closed while you do it. If you either cannot get your chin there at all, or it pulls or hurts to get there, you have just identified a problem.

Once you feel okay again, stay seated and bring your head back as far as you can to look at the ceiling. STOP if you feel any dizziness or discomfort on this one. Again, you should have been able to go back far enough to look at the ceiling directly over your head, without any discomfort. If not, you have just identified a problem.

Next, again once you feel okay, turn your head as far as you can to the right, and then to the left and see if you can turn your head the same both ways. Be aware of any tightness or stiffness you may feel. If you can't get full range both sides, or one just feels stiffer than the other, then you have just identified a problem.

Lastly, as before, once you feel okay, bring your right ear straight over and down towards your right shoulder, as far as you can. Don't cheat by bringing your shoulder up to meet your ear. Think about how if feels. Now, straighten up and bring your left ear down to your left shoulder, think about how that feels and compare how the two sides felt. Any problems?

All ranges should be full and even, if they're not, and you've never had an injury to your neck, chances are you've got some form of postural adaptation going on. So, start figuring it out and start changing things.

If those movements were painful, you may need some professional assistance in the form of physiotherapy, or chiropractic treatment to help while you are doing your home exercises, at least in the initial stages. The point it, don't delay. Take care of things before they get worse. *Listen* to what your body is telling you.

If, at this point you're thinking, "Yeah my neck is stiff or sore but it always has been," or "My doctor says I'm just getting old," or "I know it's a problem but I'm too busy right now to do much about it," then the message of this book just hasn't sunk in for you. It's your body, and now you hopefully know a lot of things about it that you didn't know before. That knowledge gives you power, right? With that knowledge comes responsibility. You have to own your problem now and take control of it if you are serious about improving your outlook. As we know, "The best time to plant a tree was forty years ago, the next best time is NOW!" You can't change what has been happening to your body up to this point, but you can change things forever from this moment on!

Now you know how to check the neck and pay attention to what you discover, I'll illustrate how listening to your body, and finding a health professional who will listen to you is a major factor in injury and disability prevention.

Case Study: The disabled **Postal Worker** who wasn't!

When "John" was sent to see me he was a mess! He had been working for his employer for ten years. Over that time he had developed chronic back pain, chronic neck and shoulder pain, debilitating headaches, and was in danger of losing his job as he could not even perform the modified duties available. X-rays and other tests had shown nothing conclusive as to why he was having these troubles, so he had been sent for psychiatric evaluations.

John's family life was deteriorating under the pressures and his pains were increasing by the month despite various medications. He was one hurting, frustrated, angry, and desperate young man. When he first came to see me, he felt that management had forced him into attending and was suspicious and hostile in his approach. Gradually he understood that I was not there to start another course of treatment, but was there to listen to what he had to say. John felt that throughout his years of increasing disability, no one had every really listened to him. So, for his first two visits, all he did was review his symptoms and vent his frustration. He had been in fine health and the first symptoms he remembered getting was shin splints in both legs, which seemed resistant to treatment. Then, gradually, he developed low back pain and progressed to the full list of problems he now suffered with.

His job consisted of taking packages from in front of him and placing them onto various shelves to each side of him. I asked him if I could watch him do this and he and his employer readily agreed for us to go into the work site. John went through the motion of lifting and placing these objects, and I noticed that after picking an object up and turning his upper body to the right to place the package on the shelf, his feet stayed pointing straight ahead!

Try it yourself now. Stand with your feet comfortably apart. Without moving your foot, turn your body to the right and stay there. Concentrate on what you feel in your right shin. It should start to feel tight. Now imagine doing that repeatedly for 40 hours a week. What was John's first complaint? Shin splints!

Once again, stand with your feet apart (comfortably), and turn your upper body to the right, only this time turn your right foot at the same time, pivoting on your heel so that your toes start and finish the movement facing the same direction as your body. Practice this a few times and feel how much easier it is on your shin. John had become accustomed to doing it his way, and after a while it felt good to him. So was it any wonder that the treatment he was getting wasn't solving anything? He was still banging his head against the wall and didn't know it!

Over time he lost mobility in his ankle and knee due to the repeated inflammation of these areas, so this naturally affected how he walked and along came hip and low back problems. In time these areas also lost mobility, causing the neck and shoulders more than their fair share of stress, and they added to his misery.

By working on the mobility of his ankle and knee, then his hip, back and neck, and giving him the understanding of how his problems had developed, John's problems began to diminish rapidly. The last I saw him he was returning to modified duties. I wish him well. You can be sure that his employer also learned from this experience and was watching other workers to correct their posture when necessary.

The point I have made here is three fold. First, listen to your body. Don't ignore the normal daily aches and pains. Remember there is no such thing as normal pains. Seek professional advice early! Secondly, if your prescribed treatment isn't working and you are cooperating fully with your health care provider, then change providers. Find someone who can make a difference. Lastly, when you seek help, if your health professional isn't listening to you, get out of there! You have to respect the experience and advice of your doctor or therapist, but if they're not listening or are down playing what you're telling them, then you're wasting your time and money.

This early intervention approach must also be given priority by industry as a whole. All too often I have encountered organizations who actively discourage the workers from reporting physical problems. Their methods have varied:

1) if you have an injury, write it in the accident book (but the workers know it will be held against them later),

2) bonuses are given to the area of the plant with the fewest *reported* injuries,

3) outright threat of job loss should the worker report an injury.

While these measures may produce apparent increase safety and wellness record for the organization on a short term basis, the problems continue to grow unchecked until they reach unmanageable levels for both workers and management. Trying to maintain the status quo cannot be done as there is no status quo and injury reduction must be tackled on a broad-based, ongoing early-intervention strategy to have *any* chance of prolonged and sustainable success. I will address the issue of early intervention again in the final chapter, but its relevance was important enough to introduce as this point also.

You already know how to "check the neck," so now check your back.

Stand with your back to a mirror. Turn your body to the right as far as you can (without discomfort) and look in the mirror to see how far your shoulder has turned. Now, go to the left and see if there's a difference. There shouldn't be! If there is—seek advice.

Next, face the mirror and lean your torso over to the right (without discomfort) and see how far your hand can slide down the outside of your leg. Then do the same motion to the left side and compare. Again, it should be easy to do, and both sides should be about even. If not— seek advice.

Lastly, bend forward from the waist, feel slightly apart, knees straight. You should be able to reach to at least half way down your shins. I know many people think this is just normal aging, but have been amazed to rediscover almost full range of motion following just one treatment and a few home stretches.

To sum up, if you're having pain and discomfort on a daily basis, get help. Listen to your body, and/or if you find some loss of range of motion in your neck or back (which takes about 30 seconds to check) get help. Fight the prospect of joining the *Early-Aging Work Force* as of today.

Before reading on, stand up and stretch or walk. Breathe deeply and do a few chin tucks!

# Chapter 16
# M.V.A. Pain – Here to Stay Pain?

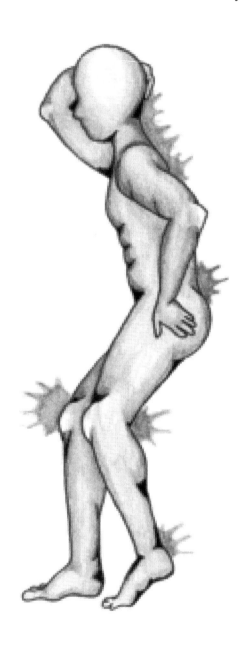

Statistics show that most of us will be involved in a motor vehicle accident (M.V.A.) of some sort or another at least once in our lifetime. The Health Costs of rehabilitation for the injuries incurred in these collisions has become massive and a cause for concern for us all.

It's not hard to see the injuries incurred in an M.V.A. could precipitate us into being one of the *Early-Aging Work Force*. The postural maladaptations discussed to this point, can and do prolong and often prevent full recovery. We'll consider how this is so, as well as a few subtle [and very common] injures that might not be receiving attention, thus delaying your recovery time!

Let's start off by looking at some of the injuries I frequently see that have not been addressed by prior health care. The majority of the M.V.A. patients I have seen have been involved in rear end collisions. That is, they were stopped in traffic and the driver behind ran into them. Symptoms of whiplash can be immediate or, more frequently, gradually increase over the following days. Neck pain, shoulder pain, headaches, pain between the shoulder blades, numbness and/or tingling of the arms and hands, are all fairly common symptoms. Clients frequently cannot understand why they have the symptoms across their shoulders and down between the shoulder blades.

Recall when we discussed the trapezius muscles (kite-shaped) and where they are situated? If not, please review that information. These patients are also unclear as to why they have numbness/tingling in their arms and hands. Remember how compression or inflammation in the neck can cause arm symptoms? So, those pains are fairly easy to explain and, with proper treatment, will mostly resolve in a relatively short period of time. More about them later.

"My wrist hurts now." "My ankle hurts now." "My low back hurts now." "My collar bone hurts now." "Nobody's doing anything about it." "No one believes these pains have anything to do with my accident because the pain only started recently." These are statements I hear all too frequently within a few weeks to a couple of months after an accident. Are these people making it up, trying to prolong their compensation claim? In most cases the answer is an emphatic NO!

First, how could they have injured their wrist? Where were their hands at the moment of impact? Either resting or braced for impact on the steering wheel. The force of the impact can compress the joints of the wrist and resulting inflammation and loss of range can produce the gradual onset of pain and decreased function. Usually mobilization and anti inflammatory modalities can resolve this problem.

How about the ankle pain? Where were their feet at the moment of impact? Either controlling or bracing for impact on the brake pedal and, possibly, the clutch. The force of the impact can compress the joints of the ankle, once again producing a gradual array of symptoms which again, can often be treated.

The low back? The force of impact also has a whiplash effect on the low back and, while the effects are usually not as immediate and dramatic as the neck, their gradual onset can be ultimately detrimental towards return to normal quality of life, if not treated promptly and properly.

I have seen clients who, because the impact was severe enough, have an apparent leg length difference since the accident, due to their body being thrown forward and their leg (braced for the impact) being pushed up into the hip joint and moving the tail bone as a result! This is a very broad picture of how this occurs, but I hope you get my meaning. You know the effects of an apparent leg length difference, now add that to the inflammation of the injuries of the accident and you can see how healing can be prolonged, and treatment often ineffective.

The collar bone pain? Remember the AC joint, where your collar bone joins your shoulder? After a M.V.A. this joint is usually inflamed and less mobile than usual because (A) that's where the seat belt dug into you at impact or (B) your arm was braced for the impact and the force was transmitted up your arm to your AC joint. Again, this is another problem which, if not identified and treated, can cause your injuries to be prolonged.

If this makes sense to you, and you or someone you know is ever in the unfortunate position of having these symptoms, make certain that your physician or therapist **listen** to you and **treat** your symptoms accordingly. I have seen patients have their wrist, ankle or back x-rayed and found to be within normal parameters, so no further action is taken. Their troubles continue, often with decreasing credibility of the patient to those providing, and also those paying for their care!

Let's go back now to the usual symptoms mentioned earlier in this chapter. We know what they are and we understand how they can come about, but other problems will inhibit healing. We must also consider pre-existing postural adaptations. Imagine I had increased curvature in my neck before the accident and didn't know I should be changing it (it felt good!) and now all my neck muscles and ligaments are inflamed and in varying degrees of spasm, while I continue to use my normal compressed posture at home and at work. I'm creating a vicious circle of pain and discomfort. How can treatment really be effective? If I already had an apparent or true leg length difference with all associated problems, how long with it take me to heal now?

While your health professionals have an obligation to listen to you and provide the best care they can, you also have an obligation and responsibility to minimize the stresses on your muscles, ligaments and joints by identifying and altering postural adaptations, as we have discussed throughout this book. Then, and only then, will you have the ideal setting for healing your injuries and to enable you to return to your normal life.

You now have knowledge that many intelligent, well-educated health care workers do not have. Frustrated with your ongoing reports of pain and disability, and unable to find specific causes, they will often recommend intensive conditioning programs where you are encouraged to work through your pain. In many cases, these gradual conditioning programs are effective, but in many others the injuries only worsen (and you know why) with the patient being told they'll just have to manage their pain, or the implication being that the patient is malingering and should be sent for a Functional Capacity Evaluation (I'll explain what that is in the next chapter).

The message is the same one I have been preaching throughout. Listen to your body, report your symptoms, demand quality care and attention, be aware of your postural adaptations, and **do** something about them. Then you will have ensured that your chances of joining the *Early-Aging Work Force* have been greatly diminished.

One problem which I haven't mention in detail is the headache in your temple(s). The majority of these headaches are associated with the jaw joint just below the temple and just about level with the base of your ear. Gentle mobilization of this joint will provide total relief from these headaches in less than 30 seconds when performed by a competent health professional. If you have this problem and no one has tried this for you, my question is, why haven't they?

Another often easily remedied pain is in the hip or upper buttock area, and is caused by a muscle called piriformis going into spasm, or just shortening over time. A simple passive stretch by your therapist is often enough to eliminate the pain completely. He or she can then instruct your spouse in the technique, and when done daily (for 30 seconds) can maintain the comfort and flexibility of your low back.

Case Study: My father.

Diagnosed with chronic hip pain (*Early-Aging Work Force*). He used to walk miles every day, but now could not walk more than 200 yards and had a handicap sticker on his vehicle. I hadn't seen my father for five years and was shocked to see him when he and my mother came to visit me in Canada eight years ago. Almost reluctantly, he agreed to let me try the piriformis stretch but was amazed at the immediate relief he felt when we did it.

Conclusion: My mother did the stretch on him when necessary, and he has had minimal recurrence of the problem.

If you have this type of pain and no one has tried this for you, why haven't they?

Another point of interest is that many patients are mentally shaken up after a motor vehicle accident and the ongoing effects of this can delay musculoskeletal rehabilitation. I have seen grown men (e.g., truck drivers) suddenly break down in tears when they revisit their wrecked vehicle or return to the site of the accident. This is a form of post traumatic stress disorder which is well recognized and for which there is appropriate treatment should the patient seek help.

When you are driving along, planning your day and within seconds your body experiences a life-threatening situation, there MUST be an effect on you mentally and emotionally. This is not speculation. This is a scientifically proven fact. I could write a whole book on this issue alone. For those of you who recognize themselves as in this category (or someone you know) I urge you to recognize that the ongoing feelings of fear and/or anger are in fact normal responses to what you have experienced. Knowing that there are many ways available to resolve these issues, often very quickly, I encourage you to discuss these matters openly with your physician and therapists as, often your family may not understand what you are going through and cannot be there for you in the ways you most need them at this time. It is not a sign of weakness to be able to discuss these things; rather it is a sign that you are in control of the situation; that you recognize that these feelings are a normal part of the healing process; and that you are taking steps to recover in as fast and organized a way as possible.

# Chapter 17
# Just What Are You Fit For?

The time comes, following injuries that have not resolved, when the injured worker is sent for a Functional Capacity Evaluation (F.C.E.) or Assessment. This test, usually scheduled over one or two days, is to determine your current capabilities. Generally speaking, the worker will be tested to establish his or her ability to balance, walk, stand, sit, bend, crouch, crawl, reach, climb stairs, lift, carry, and write in a normal work day. The results determine if you are fit to return to work, if you can return to modified duties, or what type of work you are capable of.

There are various protocols for testing, and all have their benefits. Several of these systems currently available are of excellent quality. My preference to date is Key Functional Assessments, Inc. from Minneapolis. Some insurance companies and compensation boards are going with the one day testing rather than two, as they are usually more cost effective and can get the results to the provider more quickly. I prefer the two day assessment as I can compare the second day's results to the first, which often gives me a good indication of the validity of the worker's symptoms. I've also found workers are frequently guarded and uncertain of what is happening on the first day, but are more relaxed and willing to try harder on the second day. It's a matter of personal choice on the part of the insurer, and there are benefits and drawbacks to both approaches.

Workers, and often their physicians, sometimes complain that their symptoms are worse following the testing. This is often unavoidable if you think about it. If my job is to determine your maximum capability, then I have to push you to your maximum effort. If any of us are given a work out which takes us to our maximum strength and endurance, the chances are pretty high we will be stiff and sore the next day, or maybe even for the next few days. If you have to go for this type of testing, recognize that you could be in some discomfort for a few days, but also remember it's usually normal and should pass fairly quickly. Sometimes patients tell me they were hurting all day at work after being tested in the morning. My question on this is "What the heck were you doing at work?" If I tested you to your maximum, surely that should be if for the day. I strongly encourage employers not to have the worker in at work, either immediately before or after the testing, as in some cases it can invalidate the results.

Many organizations still view the injured worker as a hindrance, and often view their symptoms as fake. I have repeatedly seen that people are basically honest, and a little respect goes a long way. So to those organizations my advice is quite simple . . . SMARTEN UP! A good F.C.E. however will catch anyone who is exaggerating his or her injuries with the hope of obtaining ongoing disability payments. Quite objectively and despite the person's best efforts, the test will uncover the deception, and the results will usually stand up in court, if necessary. This applies only to a small minority of people. Most people are genuinely hurting and all they want is to get their former life back. They deserve the best effort and respect we can give them, and this book is meant to help them.

How does the F.C.E. tie in with the *Early-Aging Work Force*? We'll look at this in two parts. First, the assessment, and secondly, how the worker got to that point.

By the time most workers come to be scheduled for a F.C.E., there are under currents of frustration, mistrust, and frequently anger. The worker feels he or she is not getting better, his or her quality of life is nowhere near what it used to be, he or she feels that his or her colleagues, employers or family are no longer sure that the disability is genuine. The worker views the assessor as a tool of their employer, insurance company or compensation board, and is sure the test is only being done to give those people the results most beneficial to them.

The employer, insurance company, or compensation board is often equally frustrated with their client's lack of progress despite exhaustive and expensive attempts at rehabilitation and they are now trying to establish what type of work the worker can do, and then get the worker doing it. It is in this environment that F.C.E.'s often are completed, and the injured worker often feels trapped with little hope of relief from their pain, although at least they can hope for gainful employment which will not make their discomfort worse. Once the person's safe levels of work are established, the person is unlikely to be coerced into doing work her or she is not capable of or which would make his or her discomfort worse. The one thing the worker knows for sure is that, unless he or she can perform to the former occupational requirements, he or she has just become a part of the statistic of the *Early-Aging Work Force*.

How did most of these people get to that point? It has repeatedly frustrated me to realize when I assess the patient and review his or her history, that topics such as neural adhesions, decreased mobility in AC joints, leg length difference, and postural adaptations, to mention but a few, have never been addressed. Again and again some simple mobilizations and stretches would have decreased the patient's pain and limited the loss of function. Sustained proper treatment is now necessary and the system is often reluctant to throw more money down a well that has, so far been unproductive, so the conflict continues.

Most of these people would not be coming for an F.C.E. had they received due and accurate care in the early stages of their disabilities. You now know that if you are injured you would relate ALL of your symptoms to your physician or therapist and make sure that they were ALL being addressed. Plus, you would do all you could to minimize the effects of postural adaptations, wouldn't you?

You are now able to identify and discuss problems with your medical advisors. You now have control over the outcome of many problems, right? I hope so. You have the knowledge, now use the power it gives you. Identify your postural adaptations. Do something about them. Discuss them with your colleagues, employers, physician and/or therapist, and take steps to prevent yourself from joining the *Early-Aging Work Force*.

Breathe, stretch, and do a few chin tucks before going on.

# Chapter 18
# The Good, The Bad, and the Just Plain Ugly!

While some organizations are making genuine efforts to prevent injuries and help their people in any way they can to maintain a healthy, safe lifestyle, to date few are successful. The reasons they aren't successful lie in what you have read to this point.

All of the ergonomic changes in a workplace and safety tips can only be effective if a person participates by complying with company policies AND identifying and altering his or her postural adaptations. In the final analysis, you are the only one who can successfully prepare for and avoid the *Early-Aging Work Force*, **and** you have to accept this responsibility, **and** act on your newly acquired knowledge. The combination of a thoughtful, caring management and an educated, responsible work force will drastically reduce injuries and disabilities. That is to everyone's benefit—ESPECIALLY YOURS!

Other organizations are what I consider to be the bad and the just plain ugly. Judge for yourself.

Example A: An industry with a huge incidence of carpal tunnel disability.

This industry was going through the motions of annually accepting help from the Compensation Board with ergonomics, but with little or no reduction in the overall injury rate. When I discussed implementing the postural adaptation awareness program with this company's C.E.O., this was his response: "Bottom line? I don't give a @#*^! I hire these people at $7.50/hour. By the time they're disabled, they're making $9.00/hour. Once they're disabled, I can get rid of them and hire somebody else for $7.50/hour."

This is scary stuff. The boss didn't see the injuries as necessarily being bad for business.

Example B: While trying to implement a prevention program, I was told by management: "Don't mention the words 'carpal tunnel' or by tomorrow they'll all say they have it."

This example shows total mistrust and lack of respect for the work force, and a complete absence of caring about increasing their workers' ability to avoid becoming part of the *Early-Aging Work Force.*

Example C: A medium -sized company (400+ employees) had a worker off due to a carpal tunnel injury.

The worker recovered quickly, but when he returned to work he was told: "You don't fit our personnel requirements. You don't work here any more!"

What message did this send to the rest of the work force? If you go off work with a compensation injury, you'll be fired! Surprise, surprise, no further injuries have been **reported** and the organization has a great record for safety. Many workers in this plant are hurting and moving rapidly towards chronic disability, but are too afraid of losing their jobs to tell anyone about their injuries!

Example D: A large industrial plant offered an excellent light-duties, return-to-work program for injured workers, to provide a worker a safe, early return to the work force and to minimize the company's no-time-loss claims.

The problem was that the workers were replaced while recovering, so when they were ready to return to full duties, they were laid off. This modified -duties system quickly became known as the "Death Line" to the work force and, once again, workers became very reluctant to report injuries of any kind. We all know where that road will end for them!

Example E: An industry with a high injury rate advises middle managers they will be paid bonuses if their area has no claims. Upper management in this company has a policy of denying all repetitive strain injuries where possible. The end product is, again, a work force with no real hope in sight as the injuries will continue, but go largely unreported. Without the type of education contained in this book, neither the management nor the workers have a chance of identifying and controlling the problems.

Example F: This is one company's policy: "Workers injured while not wearing proper safety equipment will be fined. First offense will result in 2 days lost pay. Second offense: 4 days lost pay."

This seems a reasonable request until you learn that workers who sprained their ankles while not wearing their hard hats were being penalized! Then the company stated that if injuries didn't decrease, they would contract out the work to private companies and the present employees would all be fired! Instead of dealing with the problems, the management was simply telling workers to make it go away—without giving them access to information which could help them do that!

Example G: Several years ago a large utility corporation in the U.S.A. adopted the philosophy that "there is no such thing as a false injury" and encouraged workers to voice their concerns and injuries. They also tried to gain access to the best medical help available for their people. Within a year the corporation was showing a marked decrease in time loss claims and, just as importantly, had a happy and loyal work force who recognized their employer had a *genuine* concern for their welfare.

Example H: Imagine that your injury claim has been denied, as it has been determined that you had a pre-existing condition. This is an interesting and seemingly increasing response to injury claims. While there may be a history of previous injury to the same area, unless there is medical evidence to prove that there was joint or tissue damage of a long standing nature, this is an area which will be strongly contested in many cases.

If the old injury is being blamed for the new injury, then those insurance companies or compensation boards who accepted that initial injury should now again be responsible.

Where will this all end? Since, as mentioned in the earlier chapters, postural maladaptations began as far back as our school days, then we all come to our chosen occupation with some degree of pre-existing conditions, don't we?

These examples are just a small cross section of practices in the working world. It's clear you can't always rely on your employers to act in your best interest. The only person who can help is you! Understand the message of this book and act on the advice given. Discuss the results with family, colleagues, middle management, union representatives, and upper management to work towards solutions, but let it begin with **YOU!**

It would be wonderful if we could all work together and follow the example of the American Union of Fire Fighters, who have worked hard to develop a Joint Labour/Management Initiative in injury reduction and management for their membership. They are an example to all of us and are to be applauded for their efforts, which will pay off in a happier, healthier work force with a huge saving in injury and disability costs to their employers.

# *Chapter 19*
# Corporate Cooperation

This chapter is offered as a means of helping corporations who are frustrated at the limited success of injury -reduction programs they have previously implemented. It is also offered to those employers previously addressed as the bad and the ugly in the hope that they can see the benefits, both to their work force and the corporation. It has been my experience that traditional programs in industry have proven largely ineffective in terms of injury reduction. And this is despite some excellent education in body mechanics and often expensive over hauls of the work site.

What has gone wrong? Instead of having the problem solved, what has happened is that now management feels (**a**) they wasted their money, and probably (**b**) the work force requires more supervision as they can't be following the guidelines of the program. The work force, on the other hand, feel the program was a waste of time and the ergonomic changes have made minimal impact on reducing the stresses of their job. Therefore, the problem must be with management, who expects them to work way too hard and must ultimately be responsible for their aches, pains, and injuries.

The rolling effect of all this is ongoing conflict between management and the work force, plus a degree of cynicism towards further prevention programs. Some companies feel their employees are simply not fit enough for the job and have organized daily fitness classes. They're getting closer to the root of the problem now, but generic exercise classes have actually created injuries by triggering latent problems in the work force, and with all you now know from reading this book, you can understand why.

To clarify this point again: If yours is a new company and all of your employees are screened prior to job placement—with potential physical problems identified and corrective measures implemented— then the ergonomic changes and body mechanics education will undoubtedly be cost effective. However, when you have an experienced work force in place, with all of their postural adaptations already well established, then the problem becomes almost guaranteed to be unresolvable by use of current methods. We know that everyone, including yourself, has adapted to their work site and their daily job requirements. We also know that most of us will quickly reject new techniques in body mechanics because they don't feel good to us. The few who faithfully follow the new postural requirements to the letter frequently become the next ones to be injured! So, what's happened? Simple. We know that the work force's muscles and connective tissue have shortened up in certain areas to accommodate the repetitive requirements of the job. Now they're told to do it differently and their bodies tell them it doesn't feel good. So, they either go back to their old ways, which sooner or later will create an injury, or they will persist in the new methods, resulting in injury due to their adaptations! Not exactly a win-win situation, is it?

Therefore, what **has** to happen is that the postural maladaptations have to be **identified** and **understood** by the work force. The workers have to realize that management can only solve a part of the problem with ergonomics. They then have to grasp that these postural maladaptations are the ultimate cause of many injuries and disabilities. They further have to see how they are using these same maladaptations in the home and social environment for more than they realized, so the cumulative stresses on their bodies is not just happening at work, and that the real danger is it feels good. If you have read this book and followed its guidance, then you have already achieved the goals we have just discussed. The obligation is now firmly on management to do its part to assist the workers in a joint venture for a healthier, more productive work force.

Step One: Job Requirements

A company should have fairly detailed descriptions of job demands for their workers. I have frequently found these to be outdated, inaccurate, and consequently useless as a tool in returning injured workers safely to the work force and for pre-placement screening to determine the worker's capability of performing the required tasks with minimal risk of injury.

Step Two: Light Duties

Having established an accurate list of job demands, the next step is to document which tasks that workers could safely accomplish while recovering from injury, therefore minimizing time loss claims and maintaining worker attendance and productivity.

Step Three: Work Site Analysis

Work-site analysis is a study of the work environment itself and will give such data as the heights of work surfaces, the type, style and weight of tools required to perform the tasks, and the types and frequency of movements required to fulfill the duties. There will also be a list of suggested ergonomic changes to produce a safer work environment.

**NOTE:** While many companies have implemented remedial changes, it would seem that few added the essential ingredient necessary for accuracy and success, that is: LISTEN TO YOUR WORKERS! ASK THEM WHAT THE JOB REQUIREMENTS ARE—THEY'LL TELL YOU—THEY DO IT EVERY DAY! You may be responsible for the final product, but they are the nuts and bolts of your organization and have intimate knowledge of their role. I guarantee that, if you listen to them, you'll be well on your way to a successful injury-reduction program. I have seen hundreds of job descriptions supplied by employers which, when the workers read them, cause scorn and disbelief, because what management thinks is required is nowhere close to what the employees **know** is required of them on a daily basis. Paying attention to workers' findings is a vital component of any successful wellness program.

Another necessity is to LOOK FOR EMPLOYEE ADAPTATIONS! There are many lessons to be learned from watching how workers have adapted their own work site, for example, the extra cushion or pillow in the chair, the phone book being used as a footrest or placed under the computer monitor, the use of tape to give a better, thicker grip on tools. These and many others will show you probable areas needing ergonomic review.

Step Four: To identify existing problems in the work force

Each employee would participate in a physical check of his or her kinetic chain as outlined in earlier chapters to identify problems, and each worker given suggestions what corrective measures he or she must take to decrease their potential risk of injury.

Each employee will have a follow up screening after ninety days to ensure that they have complied with the instructions given to them. To obtain worker compliance with this, confidentiality in their history is essential. In these scenarios I recommend that all workers are identified to management only by use of an individual number when the overall results of the program are presented.

Step Five: Pre-employment Placement

All potential employees would be screened as in Step Four, with the ninety day probationary period to confirm compliance with the program.

Step Six: Supervisor Training

Train the Trainer sessions are essential for supervisors and middle management. These sessions are designed to ensure these people are not only well -versed in the job requirements of the workers they supervise, but are also aware of correct use of body mechanics and **potential postural maladaptations** along with the required preventative exercises.

With the workers now able to discuss potential problems with the supervisors and the supervisors reporting monthly to upper management, plus the added factor that repeated noncompliance by a worker may become grounds for disciplinary action, we now have a system which has a chance of success.

Step Seven: Quality Assurance

With such a reporting mechanism in place, management need only identify and implement **necessary** ergonomic changes, while monitoring the success in terms of decreased injury and absenteeism with their associated costs, plus hopefully overall increased productivity. If one particular area of the work force has not shown improvement, it is relatively simple to focus on that area and identify if it is a question of poor ergonomics, inadequate supervisor awareness/participation, or noncompliance in the work force, and then act accordingly.

Step Eight: Implement ongoing health/wellness inservices and programs.

This should be looked at on three fronts. First, ask yourself if your workers are receiving adequate medical attention. Do the physicians and therapists truly understand the needs of the work force and your organization? Interview physicians and rehab personnel using some of the concepts described in this book. Are they willing to maintain a high level of communication with you to identify and resolve problems? It may be difficult to find the right people, but I assure you that it will be worth your while. Your organization will benefit while your work force will also appreciate your efforts in helping them to gain access to such people.

Secondly, identify the problems in your organization and prepare a plan of appropriate in-services for yourselves and your workers, based on your organizational needs and *not* just because the marketing tells you that the in-service is vital. Research the history of each group who offers you this kind of service. Ask for references on previous work done and *contact* the references to verify the degree of success and practicality of these programs.

Thirdly, ask the workers what type of education they feel should be given next. You'll find these answers enlightening and overall beneficial in choosing the direction for your organization.

Step Nine: Appreciate the efforts of your work force!

Show the workers how much you appreciate their compliance with the program. This does not have to be of a monetary nature (though I'm sure they wouldn't refuse it!) but can be in the form of regular updates as to how the program is progressing, while always stressing that it is only through joint management/labor participation that success was achieved.

Step Ten: Maintain the ongoing postural awareness and make it a permanent part of your corporate philosophy.

Only you, the corporation, know the true cost to your organization of your current injuries and absenteeism. You now have the inexpensive tools to greatly decrease those costs while making a huge step forward in the prevention of future costs.

I'll end with the same advice I have given to the workers throughout this book. If it makes sense, try it! What have you got to lose? Not a lot. You're already losing this battle. What do you stand to gain? Everything!

# Chapter 20
# Early Intervention

I have made many references throughout this book to the need for the work force to identify their aches and pains at an early stage and to seek professional help as soon as possible. This maxim applies equally so at the corporate level. Make sure you have a system in place where your worker receives the best possible medical care **as soon as possible** following an injury, to facilitate prompt accurate diagnosis and correct treatment for a safe, early return to work. This type of intervention is **absolutely essential** in disability prevention. As I said earlier, the majority of patients I have seen attending for Functional Capacity Evaluations have been "disabled" for prolonged periods of time. The frustration is that if proper early intervention had been implemented, these patients would not have been sitting in front of me and the costs of their rehabilitation would be minute in comparison to their ongoing disability.

Everybody seems to be looking at technology as the answer to our problems. We expect the medical system to be able to fix all of our complaints, after all we are in a new millennium, aren't we? Yet we are all frustrated with the health care system's inability to correct our problems, and the medical system is equally frustrated with us! So what is currently happening is that costs for our care are spiraling, a massive rehabilitation industry is getting richer, but we're not getting better and somehow we're being blamed for it all!

Now you know now a lot of it was your fault, but you didn't know how you could have done things any differently! You were "banging your head on the wall" and didn't know it, so how could you be expected to change. But now you understand how you are contributing to the problems and you know what to do about it, and what others should do about it. The message has been simple and often repeated, so I'm sure you've got it by now. Unfortunately, you cannot predict that others will do their best to help you. However you have taken responsibility for your own actions by reading this book. My advice is read it again and again until you fully understand the parts you need to know. Share your knowledge and discuss it with others. Fight and Avoid joining the *Early Aging Work Force*.

With my best wishes to all of you for a long, happy and healthy life!

~ Hugh

# Author Profile

Hugh Gilbert is a Physical Therapist, Published Author, International Speaker and Lecturer educated initially in Glasgow, Scotland and after 35 years in Canada has returned to teach in the U.K. while still teaching throughout North America and has taught in Mexico, Argentina and Hawai'i. Hugh is also a Registered Independent Medical Consultant and Advanced Myofascial Therapist. His amazing protocol "Kinetic Chain Release" is his Intellectual Property and has been accepted for Continuing Education Credits by The Scottish Massage Therapy Association; The Irish Physical Therapy Association; The Missouri Physical Therapy Association; The Canadian Sports Massage Therapists Association; The Arizona School of Integrated Studies; and The Alberta Association of Massage Therapists. Hugh was a keynote speaker at the World Conference of Complementary Medicine in Santa Fe and has been an assistant instructor at the Presentation of Myofascial Release to the American Back Society Conference in Orlando. During this time, Hugh gained extensive insights over the years as a trusted consultant to industry and insurance companies. Over the last 3 decades, he has maintained balance in his education in other ways, much of his interest directed towards not only industry but also sports, culminating in five years as Head Coach at University level in Canada He is grateful for the invaluable experience gained by involvement in other areas such as the Skate Canada Championships and the Canadian National Basketball Championships.

In other areas, Hugh has been an ongoing student of and now a recognized International Teacher of Energy Work; Hawaiian Healing Studies; Celtic Healing; Native American Studies; is an Ordained Minister of Spiritual Peacemaking, and has presented Interfaith Workshops. He has successfully implemented conflict resolution startegies for families and corporations.. Much of Hugh's recent work has evolved around success working with Autistic and Attention Deficit children, their parents, teachers and caregivers.

These areas were not addressed in this particular publication as the focus here is clearly about physical dysfunction and will deal with this from a purely structural/functional perspective. For more information on workforce or any other areas of interest please contact Hugh at

**www.kineticchainrelease.com**
**www.hughgilbertauthor.com**
**www.hughgilbert5D.com**
or email at **yahugh@journeysend.ca**

It is Hugh's mission to offer Peace Through Healing to the world in as many ways and places as possible. This book is dedicated to that end and is specifically directed to the Workforce and Industrial Arena. The goals of this book are primarily to offer solutions to injured workers in ways they had never dreamed possible, and present these solutions in a simple, easy and logical manner, improving and often restoring their functional capabilities, their confidence, their self esteem and their capacity to earn a living. To further educate and empower these workers through the contents of this book in understanding how their issues arose and how to minimize the chances of recurrence. This policy, as it takes hold in the work force, will then automatically impact on and reduce national injury, absenteeism and disability rates and costs which currently are a cause of major concern to Industry; Municipal, State and Federal Governments and Insurance Companies.

This book offers the solution based means of early identification, intervention and resolution of potential disability, not only in the workforce, but in schoolchildren and athletes. The information given is meant to present Problem Solving and Conflict Resolution possibilities empowering to all parties, in the workplaces (and many homes) of the nation.

During his time working with industrial injuries, Hugh has consistently analyzed the problems facing the work force and identified areas needing improvement. He developed a Functional Capacity Evaluation based on finding solutions to the workers physical problems and not just their perceived inadequacies in the area of job requirements, and has recently developed and implemented a revolutionary assessment protocol for Pre-Placement Screening for workers which is non confrontational; solution focussed; and results and satisfaction driven: with outstanding and exciting results giving hope and relief to many individuals who lived in apprehension that they were showing signs of oncoming inability to continue in their chosen line of work. The cost effectiveness of this programme is attracting the attention of Industry and Insurance Companies as Hugh has created a scenario where "everyone wins."

His rehabilitative program for those who have not responded well to traditional rehabilitation has proven highly successful, and he is currently marketing this service internationally.

Hugh believes the medical profession, in general, still do not take— or are given—enough time to listen to their patients and act accordingly, and also that if they did have that time to listen, many of our injured workers' problems would be resolved. He further believes that physicians and rehabilitation practitioners should be better trained to meet the needs of the injured worker and of industry. "The current approach to injury reduction needs to be completely reconsidered. Medical practitioners must (1) Be given an understanding of current Corporate and Union philosophies, and the negotiating skills to allow alignment with both to create a safer work environment; (2) Be educated in industry specific postural adaptations; (3) Understand the premise of how Return to Work and Light Duties Programmes are often detrimental to injury resolution. (4) Be taught the premise contained in this book and consequently be able to recognize and understand the impact of maladaptation in the kinetic chain on their patients and know how to quickly correct such adaptations; incorporating these corrections into current treatment programmes."

"My studies and experience have brought me to the clear conclusion that Postural Awareness and Kinetic Chain Release are the ultimate keys to injury reduction we have long awaited, while I honour and applaud the progress made in Workplace Safety I feel that many of the current *Exercise*, *Ergonomic* and *Injury Reduction* programmes have proven to have limited success in that there are Tens of Thousands of workers—both diagnosed and undiagnosed—who are physically, and/or, emotionally, and/or mentally suffering, in many cases unable to perform the meaningful work of choice; with the corresponding loss of self esteem and income and that a high percentage of these workers can greatly decrease their pain levels and increase their functional capabilities dramatically through understanding and acting on the contents of this book and that, ultimately only the workers themselves, individually and collectively, have the power to change their future. My hope is that I have offered them the necessary tools in this simple publication."

Once again Hugh may be contacted by email at:
**yahugh@journeysend.ca**

Made in the USA
Charleston, SC
11 March 2014